DEION SANDERS

WITH DON YAEGER

FOREWORD BY JOHN C. MAXWELL

ELEVATE AND DOMINATE
21 WAYS TO WIN ON AND OFF THE FIELD

GALLERY BOOKS/13A

New York   London   Toronto   Sydney   New Delhi

Gallery Books/13A
An Imprint of Simon & Schuster, LLC
1230 Avenue of the Americas
New York, NY 10020

First 13A/Gallery Books hardcover edition March 2024

13A is a trademark of Charles Suitt and is used with permission.

GALLERY BOOKS and colophon are registered trademarks of Simon & Schuster, LLC

Simon & Schuster: Celebrating 100 Years of Publishing in 2024

For information about special discounts for bulk purchases, please contact Simon & Schuster Special Sales at 1-866-506-1949 or business@simonandschuster.com.

The Simon & Schuster Speakers Bureau can bring authors to your live event. For more information or to book an event, contact the Simon & Schuster Speakers Bureau at 1-866-248-3049 or visit our website at www.simonspeakers.com.

Interior design by Davina Mock-Maniscalco

Manufactured in the United States of America

10 9 8 7 6 5 4 3 2 1

Library of Congress Cataloging-in-Publication Data

Names: Sanders, Deion, author. | Yaeger, Don, author.
Title: Elevate and dominate : 21 ways to win on and off the field / Deion Sanders, with Don Yaeger.
Description: First 13A/Gallery Books hardcover edition. | New York : Gallery Books /13A, [2024].
Identifiers: LCCN 2023051342 | ISBN 9781668026793 (hardcover) | ISBN 9781668026816 (ebook)
Subjects: LCSH: Success.
Classification: LCC BF637.S8 S259 2024 | DDC 650.1 — dc23/eng/20231107
LC record available at https://lccn.loc.gov/2023051342

ISBN 978-1-6680-2679-3
ISBN 978-1-6680-2681-6 (ebook)

This book is dedicated to
Jimmie Callaway, Ron Hoover, Dave Capel,
Mims Sanders, Willie Knight, and Bishop Omar Jahwar,
the men who helped shape my journey.

CONTENTS

FOREWORD

JOHN C. MAXWELL

Leaders fascinate me. I've spent more than four decades study-ing the principles of the greatest leaders, who inspire the masses and change lives. It's a timeless gift and we all need to learn those lessons.

Some of the best leaders are coaches who command a pres-ence while rallying their teams around the focus of a great cause and creating the discipline that makes them better people.

I'll tell you this without qualification: I want Deion Sanders—Coach Prime himself—to be my coach!

As you read through these pages filled with Deion's magical mix of life experience, common sense, and driven motivation, I think you'll reach the same conclusion.

Anyone who follows sports knows Deion Sanders to be one of the greatest athletes of our time. Some of his accomplishments seem like they were crafted by a Hollywood screenwriter, but I can assure you they are all true.

What I love about Deion is how he refused to rest on those very significant laurels. He has an unquenchable desire to keep learning and keep improving as a person. The most beautiful part is how he discovered his voice.

He's a coach. He's a leader of people. He's an observer of human nature and a man who's going to shoot it straight, because he knows that honesty is the starting point of how we all get better.

You're going to hear about Deion's outstanding athletic career in this book, but only as a means to teach more important lessons. This isn't the predictable story of a legendary sports figure recounting his triumphs. He shows us ALL how to find our own glory days. Among the special treats offered by Deion:

- Ways to become a better spouse, parent, or friend

- The path to career fulfillment

- The challenge of working toward the life you've always imagined

I believe everyone can benefit from a mentor. So how do you find one? What are you really seeking? Someone who is *really good*, right? Deion Sanders has proven to be stellar in his field. People do what people see. What Deion has accomplished in reinvigorating Jackson State, and the captivating turnaround we're witnessing at Colorado, tells you all you need to know about his abilities to organize, teach, and lead.

About fifteen years ago, Deion Sanders called me out of the blue. He had picked up one of my books at an airport and he felt like he was really helped by the things he read. I was going to be in Dallas for a conference, so he invited me to his home so we could visit and watch Monday Night Football.

Before the visit, I had arranged for a few of my latest leadership books to be sent to his home. When I landed in Dallas and started to head toward his home, my agent at the time, David Hoyt, suggested we stop at a Walmart on the way to pick up about a dozen footballs so Deion could sign them for us.

Well, once we got there, I first offered to sign the books I had sent his way. He just said, "No, I wouldn't ask you to do that. I'm sure people ask you to sign things all the time. They just want to make sure they can show other people they met you. I don't want anything from you except your presence and the chance to learn from you."

I guess there was a lesson for me. The most valuable thing we can give someone isn't our autograph or any material thing for that matter. It's our human connection, the ability to relate and find common ground, the honest desire to teach someone a better way and help their life. And what a humble spirit Deion showed while teaching me that lesson!

Needless to say, those footballs never made it out of my car. In fact, we were back at Walmart later that night to return them! But that night began a great relationship. For hours upon hours, we talked about leadership and life in general. I remember Deion occasionally checking out the TV, assessing the game, complaining that somebody missed a coverage, or pretty much predicting what was coming next.

Even then, he was coaching.

It's interesting to me how Deion, even after one of the most distinguished careers in NFL history, has developed an even greater desire to teach and mentor young people. That's something I've always noticed about highly successful people. It's more satisfying for them to have a positive impact on somebody's life and watch them do well.

Deion already knows what he accomplished—and it was considerable. Now he has discovered how much more he can do through others.

The best football players in America want to be coached by Deion Sanders. Through this book, we're fortunate that Deion can now coach all of us . . . even those who don't care a bit about football.

Get ready to find out about Deion. And get ready to learn a lot more about yourself in the process.

As someone who is endlessly fascinated by leaders, I can't wait to see Deion's coaching path unfold because I know every step will be memorable.

John C. Maxwell is a *New York Times* bestselling author, executive coach, and speaker who has sold more than forty million books in fifty languages.

Why Coach Prime Should Be YOUR Coach!

Hey baby, it's Coach Prime. Thanks for picking up my book. Let's cut to the chase. Here's how this is gonna go down. I don't want to lecture. Let's have a real conversation. That's so much better. That's so much more intimate. I'm guessing you're interested in this book because you're looking for ANSWERS. That's why you're here, right? Well, we'll get to those in a little bit. But first, I got a few questions for YOU.

Do you feel like the BEST PARTS of life are just passing you by?

Are you spending most of your time just WORRYING?

Do you HATE going to work every morning?

Have you forgotten what it's like to have a TRUE PASSION for the things you're involved in?

Do you still have DREAMS?

When your head hits the pillow every night, are you at PEACE?

When you look in that mirror, do you LIKE what you see?

DO YOU HAVE A PLAN AND WHAT IS IT?

How do you ATTACK your days?

Let's get this straight. I AM A COACH. I want to be YOUR coach. So, what we need off the rip is a game plan.

We're going to lay out twenty-one ways—that's right, twenty-one ways . . . you do know I wore 21, right?—for you to win on and off the field. If you follow this plan, it's gonna ELEVATE you in every area of your life. And when you ELEVATE, that means you're ready to DOMINATE.

This is my formula. This is how I work. When I became head coach of the Colorado Buffaloes in 2023, I took over a team that was 1–11. Many people openly mocked us, ridiculed us, DOGGED US. They told us what we could be, weren't gonna be, and ain't gonna be. But I knew we were gonna turn it around and make things happen.

When they started to see the results, the skeptics were tripping all over themselves to proclaim how great the Colorado uprising was for college football. It was fine with me. That was cool with me. To me, there was never any doubt whatsoever. Just like how I have no doubt you'll be successful if you just follow the game plan for ELEVATION and DOMINATION. It has worked before. It's gonna work again for YOU.

There are still LOTS of people who don't believe in themselves—period. So believing in what we've got going at Colorado was far-fetched. They think it's some sort of mirage or magic trick. They can't accept it because it doesn't fit into that safe little box of how things have always been done.

Folks are entitled to their opinions, but I really don't care. Because their opinion of me is not the opinion I have of myself.

How you gonna argue with facts, man?

For the first time in twenty-seven years, the Colorado season tickets were sold out. Gone! And that was just FOUR MONTHS after we were hired, long before our first game. Our Colorado Buff Club had raised nearly $30 million in donations and was on track to DOUBLE what they'd brought in the previous year. They tell me EVERY home game we had in Boulder was worth approximately $20 million in economic impact for our community.

Our late-night overtime victory against Colorado State became the fifth-most-watched college football game of all time on ESPN (9.3 million viewers). Even after 2 a.m. on the East Coast, when our game was still going, we had more than 8 million viewers (and that was more than 1 million larger than the peak audience of any college football game that week).

Colorado football was featured on ESPN's *College GameDay*, Fox's *Big Noon* pregame show, the *Today* show, *CBS This Morning*, and *60 Minutes*. *Time* magazine featured my smiling face on its cover with the headline "THE BELIEVER: How Deion Sanders Is Changing Football Forever."

That's a lot.

We must be doing something right and we're only gonna continue. Keep in mind, we're only gonna get better . . . and better . . . and better.

Winning games. Leading young men and positively impacting their lives. Changing the face of not only a football program but an entire campus. Waking up every day full of life. Having so much fun I can hardly stand it and raising my kids simultaneously. Knowing that our future has sparkling potential. I'm definitely walking in my purpose. And that's what I want for YOU.

That's the result of our game plan. I want you in the end zone, celebrating your accomplishments. We're going after this aggressively. We're not choosing the safe route. Trust me, safe AIN'T IT! I've learned that through the years.

If I'd chosen the safe route, the average route, I'd still be leading a comfortable life, winding down each day at a nice crib on my ranch in Texas while fishing in Lake PRIME or Lake TIME.

If I'd chosen the typical route, I'd be making a few strategic appearances, private autograph signings, maybe doing some television, watching my kids play on weekends, while still building the Prime brand. But . . .

I'm not average.

And I'm sure not typical.

I was born to do what I'm doing now. I was born to coach.

While you may know me from the five different NFL teams I played on during my career, along with a pair of Super Bowl championship rings and eight trips to the Pro Bowl, that's not how you are going to remember me.

You're going to REMEMBER ME as COACH PRIME.

Because that's what God has called me to be. And I responded. That's my PASSION. That's my PURPOSE.

And I want you to find and feel the same wonderful thing.

As a coach, I'm constantly on the lookout for people of character who have the potential to be SMART, TOUGH, FAST, and DISCIPLINED WITH CHARACTER. I'm here to teach those people more than blocking and tackling, running and jumping, throwing and catching. It's my job, and my passion, to help turn and navigate them into success stories who will have an impact on this world.

So you might be thinking to yourself, *That's all well and good, Coach Prime, I get that you know how to coach football players, but why should you be MY coach?* What does Coach Prime have to offer that would help YOUR situation? What can Coach Prime bring to the table that might RESONATE in your life?

EVERYONE can benefit from a good coach. I know I have. The right coach makes you soar. Michael Jordan and Tom Brady had coaches that changed the direction and outcome of their lives. Nobody does it alone. And while you may not be number 23 or number 12 (few are), having someone to push you, remind you, MOTIVATE you, especially when you don't feel like it, will always ELEVATE your game and how you represent—yourself, your team or company, your family, and community.

A football team isn't all that different from a family, a company, or a cause. We're all after the same things—achievement, reaching our potential, improvement, togetherness, fulfillment, happiness. Me and you, we're about to take a journey together. And if you listen well enough, I promise you'll pick up some things that will help you reach your goals. We'll also even have some FUN along the way.

But first, I'll tell you right off, you have to be willing to get naked to make this happen. Yeah, you heard me. Get rid of your Blenders. Take off your hat. Kick off your shoes. Slip out of that jacket. This isn't Halloween. I don't have any treats for you. Get rid of your costume.

Now, who are we looking at?

You. That's ALL YOU, BABY. Naked and not ashamed.

I need you to strip down and get rid of the junk and baggage you're carrying. All of us are carrying some sort of luggage. In order to do this work—to be great, to be a leader—we need to look at ourselves, fully, with complete honesty. See who we are and who we may become. That's when the real progress can begin.

So, why should I be YOUR coach? Yeah, you're right. I'm flawed, shawl ain't perfect and still trying to get life right myself. Why am I writing this book? Plain and simple, I WANT YOU TO GO TO THE NEXT LEVEL. Other books have helped me. All the coaches throughout my life have helped me. I listened to them. I watched them. I learned from them. I gleaned from them. Now it's YOUR turn.

And like any good football coach, I'm going to DEMAND your attention. I love it in the military when the commander says, "ATTENTION!" And everyone snaps into place. Now, I'm literally saying "ATTENTION!" All eyes on me. None of this is going to work if you don't listen up and take notes. I'll give it to you straight and keep it 100 at all times, no chaser.

Think of me as your boxing coach, always in your corner. Between rounds, I'm going to sit you down, give you some words of wisdom while you're toweling off, get you fired up, re-energize you, pull back that chair, and send you back out to the middle of the ring.

"Left . . . right . . . left . . . right . . . OK . . . back off him . . . now go . . . you got this . . . you got this!"

Sometimes, when you're in the fight, you can't see the bigger picture. That's where I come in. I'm a FIXER. I've always been a FIXER. And I'm always gonna be a FIXER.

The Road to Coaching

I grew up in the Jones Walker Apartments in Fort Myers, Florida. We ultimately moved to 1625 Anderson Avenue. Right up the street, there was a tremendous amount of dysfunction with drug deals and so forth. They actually put a police station directly on Anderson Avenue, right on one of the main streets that ran through town.

Even at an early age, I saw a lot more for myself. My mama, Connie Knight, was working multiple jobs, trying to make the ends see one another, although they never actually met. I think I was maybe seven when I told my mama, who was raising me and my sister, Tracie, on her own, that I was going to make a lot of money one day. So much money that she would get to retire and wouldn't have to work another day in her life. I said this with GREAT CONFIDENCE.

I always believed in myself and knew I'd find a way out. Sports was my ticket. It all started back in high school, when I first became a true student of the game. Later, in the NFL, I worked and studied MY BUTT OFF and retained everything I saw. I was a man of routine who always looked to get his techniques and steps just right. We didn't have iPads back then, so I'd drag around whatever contraption I could find to watch film. I didn't have access to film like that until college, but even back in high school, I was watching and learning, watching and learning, taking in every detail I could.

Yeah, I had a lot of GOD-GIVEN ability. But the game's organization and strategy really fascinated me. It was interesting how the coaches built their team and motivated the players. In all aspects of football, I always wanted to know . . . *why?* I honestly think I had coaching on the brain even back then.

After high school, I played for Coach Bobby Bowden's Florida State Seminoles and the defensive coordinator was Mickey Andrews, one of the greatest coaches I've ever played for IN MY LIFE. Sitting in my dorm room, this agent handed me a document that stated how much money players made at each position in the NFL. That's when it all triggered.

I knew I had THE GAME. Now I had to figure out how the whole country would know MY NAME. I knew I had to go above and beyond the norm. I wanted to stand out and make some money eventually as an NFL DB. So, I came up with my "Prime Time" persona, which was based on a nickname that was given to me on the basketball court by my dear friend Richard Fain. I turned it into my alter ego, even though many people thought it was my true identity (and some still do). Muhammad Ali wasn't Ali all the time—he was Cassius Clay. Flip Wilson played Geraldine, but he wasn't like that offstage. I truly don't think I was anything like Prime Time, but I played that role for all it was worth.

Deep down, I consider myself to be soft-spoken and introverted (if you can believe that). But as Prime Time, I was on the big stage. I think we all have an alter ego of some sort, and I just became one of those people who got to play that out before a multitude of millions. That was the beginning of the Florida State football program becoming incredibly popular.

I like to think I had something to do with that level of interest. Whether you LOVED me or HATED me, you had to WATCH me.

I was told I was the only athlete to appear in the Super Bowl AND the World Series. That amazed me! I truly didn't care about things like that because I was just living my life, the same way I had since I was a kid. I played fourteen seasons in the NFL, and some people say I defined the position of cornerback. I got Super Bowl rings with the San Francisco 49ers and Dallas Cowboys. And I was also privileged to play nine seasons of major league baseball.

I've been blessed to have made it into the Pro Football Hall of Fame and the College Football Hall of Fame. While that speaks to my ability, this game is about more than talent—a lot more. I've always been driven to do and know more. I've watched more film than a *New York Times* movie critic. I've lived this game since I was a kid and that has given me the ability to see the whole field and judge talent, while also knowing instinctively what works and what doesn't. But I think the best quality I had as a player, and now have as a coach, is the ability to read people, to understand human nature, and to know where to put people so they achieve their best and the whole operation around them works better.

So, that brings me to how I went from being on the field to sitting on the sidelines, not as a player or a coach but as a FATHER. It all started in 2012, when my sons Shilo and Shedeur were twelve and ten. They were playing in a youth football league. I was sitting in the stands, just as their dad, not as an NFL player, not as a coach. But as I watched the drills, I immediately knew they were doing them all wrong. Those kids were running just ten yards apart, and somebody was gonna end up with a concussion. They at least had to be angled. I couldn't help myself; I kept getting up and correcting, getting up and correcting. I was concerned not just for my sons but for all the players on the field.

In that moment, while I had never pictured myself wearing a headset on anybody's NFL or collegiate sideline, sitting in the stands that day, watching my own kids be coached, I knew I could do things a whole lot better.

As a result, the TRUTH youth sports organization was born.

TRUTH was originally going to be one team, but because I didn't want to turn any kids away, it ended up being two teams, at ten different age levels. We had summer camps with close to six hundred kids, where they could play football, basketball, baseball, do cheer, and run track and field. We also brought in full-time tutors as well. In order to participate, the kids had to maintain a certain grade-point average, so we sent important messages from the beginning.

When I got inducted into the Pro Football Hall of Fame, we brought seven busloads of TRUTH kids and parents to the ceremony in Canton, Ohio—all different ethnicities and socioeconomic statuses, but one big family.

As I said that evening, we were raising those kids to be CEOs, not employees. Leaders, not followers. They thought we were teaching them football, which we were, but we were also teaching them life by being demanding of them on the field and in the classroom. My biggest passion, both then and now, is helping kids and getting them to a better place in life. While it was incredible to be inducted into the Pro Football Hall of Fame that night, I also knew that I could take my platform and do so much more than just parade around in my gold jacket and make a living off my name. I had lots more to give and there were so many kids out there to give it to.

I saw my coaching and mentoring role expanding, which led to the opening of the Prime Prep Academy charter schools in the Dallas area in 2012. Sadly, it closed a few short years later due to a lack of oversight (I'll get more into this with y'all in Chapter 18). That said, despite failing, I was still grateful that we were able to help as many kids as we did. The lessons I learned from this experience—mainly who to trust—I still bring forward with me to this day. I simply didn't pay enough attention to my schools and I paid a price for that.

Everybody's passion isn't YOUR passion. Everybody don't love kids the way you love kids. BE CAREFUL who you do business with. That's the main thing I gleaned from that. And I learned a lot from that time. And I know that I'm always gonna bring it back to the positive lessons I learned as a MAN and as a FATHER.

Look, it's the same principle as football. When you hit adversity, you learn from your mistakes, then you keep going. Football means so much to my life. It taught me how to get up after getting knocked down. It taught me how to play with pain. It taught me about dedication, focus, and sacrifice.

Football returns to you what you give it. The game understands what you put into it. To get the results you want, you've got to give the game some affection, attention, and consideration. It's real that way. You can't just love the game some of the time. I carry this with me no matter where I go and who I coach.

In 2017, I couldn't resist the chance to become offensive coordinator at Trinity Christian High School in suburban Dallas. I got to coach with my dear friends Kevin Mathis and Andre Hart, and we're still coaching together today. We won three Class 2A state championships, and happily for me, I got to continue coaching Shedeur and Shilo. You started to see that those kids had a big future in football—Shedeur was the quarterback and Shilo found a home at defensive back, although he also helped us at receiver.

In 2019, I went to Constance Schwartz-Morini, my business partner and manager (at SMAC Entertainment), with an idea that had been percolating in my mind. I had reached out to the athletic director at Florida State, the school where I first made my name, to see if I could help with recruiting.

"What do you mean, you want to help with recruiting?" she said. "Why would you help them recruit? Why wouldn't you just go for it and be a head coach?"

Now, you got to understand my relationship with Constance. She's brilliant. Her sense of timing is impeccable. So that concept rattled around in my brain for a few seconds and I said, "You're right. Let's go for it!"

She worked hand in hand with my longtime coach and friend Ray Forsett—"Pretty Tony" is what they call him.

Pretty Tony put a GREAT plan together and we had answers for all the questions I could be asked. We had the structure for building a staff, recruiting players, and building a program that would WIN. When I prepared for an interview, we used to joke around and tell each other, "It's not gonna be because of ME." We completely believed we would DOMINATE any interview, so there had to be some outside factor in play if we didn't get the job.

Just like that, the trajectory of my life changed completely. Instead of days upon days filled with fishing at my very comfortable home, I was going to be coaching. But for who?

I talked with FSU and Arkansas, and those interviews went very, very well. For whatever reason, both schools went in different directions and hired other head coaches. Truthfully, I was still working through the idea of coaching in my head. Honestly, it wasn't something I had been thinking about very long. It wasn't on my bucket list. When my son Shedeur initially committed to Florida Atlantic University—and he did that because of the relationship he'd established with the head coach, Willie Taggart, from his time at FSU—there was talk of them creating a different position and title for me at FAU. But I really didn't want to do that.

So how did I become a college head coach anyway?

It was Pretty Tony who first broached the subject: "Hey, have you considered an HBCU?" (That stands for Historically Black Colleges and Universities). I honestly had not.

We were still in COVID, coming off the murder of George Floyd, and Pretty Tony thought there was a HUGE opportunity for me to make an impact at an HBCU. That was all I wanted—an opportunity to coach some kids and change some lives. The more I thought about it, the more perfect it seemed.

Nobody saw me heading to Jackson State, a legendary institution that had been way, way down (four head coaches and four athletic directors in the previous eight seasons). It made no sense. I was very comfortable with my life in Dallas, but here I was being asked to enter an environment of total discomfort. I went from the peace and serenity of being at home to a situation where there was something to be solved, something to be fixed, something to be addressed first thing every day I went to work—and that was before I even got to the football part.

But I was NEEDED. So, when I got that collect call from God telling me to go where I was needed, I accepted the charges. I never looked back. This was a true challenge that spoke to my competitive side. And I knew I was going to help some kids in a big way. When you are NEEDED like that, when you have all the resources and intellect to fulfill that need, how can you say no? Especially if God placed it in your spirit.

Speaking of needs, Jackson State's football program needed SO MUCH. Everything from a turf practice field, which my friends at Walmart generously donated, to new dining arrangements that allowed the food to be brought to our football facilities instead of having to send our guys off-campus for their meals, thanks to our friends at SodexoMagic, the company founded by Magic Johnson. We got those necessities through our connections, perseverance, and the excitement and goodwill we were able to generate.

Through the uptick in donations, we got a new locker room. With help from Procter & Gamble, we also resurfaced the Jackson State tennis courts and track and field facilities. We began a Jackson State speaker series and mentorship program, thanks to my SMAC management company, which brought in CEOs and high-profile individuals from places like Aflac, Walmart, Oikos, and the NFL to talk to the students about potential careers. We even established a coding academy for computer programming training.

I'm proud of what we accomplished at Jackson State, particularly how we changed the perception of what an HBCU program is all about. *College GameDay* came to Jackson. So did *60 Minutes*. The exposure and attention were unprecedented. Oh, and we won a few games, too.

And while we were able to raise Jackson State's profile on a national level, *all* HBCUs need more television exposure, more donations from the alumni, better facilities, more engagement from the fans. Those programs have too much history and heritage to just be ignored and forgotten. While our time in Jackson was relatively short, I like to think our impact was relatively large and that because of it HBCUs will continue to draw attention and expectation.

Now, I'm pretty sure no one predicted that three years after I started at Jackson State, with a 27–6 record and two Southwestern Athletic Conference (SWAC) championships behind me, this Florida-born-and-bred kid would wind up in the mountains and cold of Boulder at the University of Colorado, a Power 5 conference school. I guess life is funny sometimes.

But coaching is coaching—whether it's Jackson State, Colorado, or the moon. It's about putting people in positions to succeed, teaching them the right way, holding them accountable, and making decisions. Now we'd been called to Colorado. And our intention was to put that program back among the ELITE and WIN—on and off the field.

Your Personal Navigation System

Sometimes the right words can make all the difference. I'm called Coach, but I also fill a need and serve as a navigational system for all kinds of people, not just players.

My life experiences have made me well equipped to deal with all sorts of football players. Professional players are getting a check. They're young men, but they're really pretty much boys with a lot of money. I can teach my college players the best way to reach the NFL.

High school kids are hungry to get to the next level. I think I have an advantage in coaching and recruiting because I was recruited, and I've also been the guy coaching in college. Plus, I've been the father of kids who were recruited and coached, so that gives me a tremendous competitive edge.

Whether it's one of my players or someone with an issue within their family or business—I'm going to lead you where you want to go. Pretend you're in my meeting room, getting ready for the big game. The game of life is as big as it gets. So we're not doing this for entertainment. This is serious stuff.

I want you to study each of the twenty-one ways to win on and off the field. Some of them you already know about. The others are maybe new concepts. This is OUR game plan. These are the rules we live by. I need you COMPLETE. I need you ALL IN. These words are gonna leap off the page and help improve your life—a LOT.

When your life ELEVATES, then you begin to DOMINATE and vice versa. I'm excited to be YOUR COACH during this time because I've seen how lives, including my own, can change from following these principles.

Coaching is about RELATIONSHIPS, TRUST, DEPEND-ABILITY, and CONNECTION. It's on me to help young people understand who they are, what they are, how they are, and where they're trying to go. Again, I help them find and follow their personal navigational system, and it's my job to get them to their destination. But it's not just my players that I am responsible for. I'm here to help YOU do the very same thing.

When I set out to write this book, my hope was that you would read it with pen in hand, taking notes, underlining key sentences, writing things in the margins. That's the way I consume my favorite books. I'm constantly underlining passages or putting stars next to important statements. I hope you underline this WHOLE BOOK. I want you to carefully read these ideas, these quotes, and these concepts. I've made sure to include five take-away points at the end of each chapter to help give you something to walk away with and think about. Let them sink in and see how they can apply to your life.

Once you read the book, you're not done. I designed it to be your constant companion. All of our lives are like roller coasters, filled with peaks and valleys. You'll want to dip into each of these twenty-one ways at various points in your life, maybe when you're feeling stuck, maybe when you need a pep talk, maybe just to give yourself confidence before taking on an important task.

This book won't sit on your shelf and collect dust. It's more like an interactive road map. You'll be reaching for it all the time.

But to truly get the most out of this book, to figure out who you really are, let's circle back to that idea of getting naked. Because you can't be wearing a COSTUME and do this kind of work.

It's OK, I'll get naked first in these pages. You'll see me at my best and my worst. You may not even recognize me at certain times. There were definitely times when I didn't recognize myself. But I'm going to be comfortable with it because there's nothing fake. It's who I am—24/7.

Because what good is it to keep wearing those fake costumes every day? It's all a myth. We are who we are. You can't be scared to find that out. When you get naked, when you're not hiding behind a costume or a false front, that's when you know who you really are in this world. And that's when you can become and do better.

I have a lot of high-profile accomplishments, but I truly believe my top plays happened back in Fort Myers, when none of you knew anything about me, when there were no cameras around. When I wasn't wearing a costume. When I was naked, and my mentality was all about . . . keep making plays.

And that's what I want you to do. When you're at the office finishing that project and everybody else has gone home, I want you to *keep making plays*. Maybe your sales numbers aren't leading the pack right now. *Keep making plays*. Nobody's talking about you.

Nobody's appreciating you. You aren't on anybody's leaderboard. *Keep making plays.*

Yes, I have made a lot of mistakes. But I've also done a lot of good—and I think I've only just begun.

I'm not average.

I'm not typical.

I don't think you are either.

I want to bring some CLARITY, PURPOSE, and PASSION to your world. So let's make this journey together, tackling this very complicated, very rewarding thing called life together. Show up for me, bring an open mind, and let's see if these things don't make a little sense to you.

After that, the next step is about becoming all you were meant to be.

Let's go!

Coach Prime
November 2023

CHAPTER 1

Even If You're Broken, Keep Moving!

As a college football coach, I'm known for a multitude of things: motivational speeches, insight, intangibles that make a football player better. I give hair-raising, provocative speeches that make my players think, move them to action, or cause them to scream out in a warrior cry.

But on that November day in 2021, as I looked into the eyes of my Jackson State team, as I reflected on my broken mindset, I couldn't find the right words. All I could do was cry.

My own kids—Deiondra, Deion Jr., Shilo, Shedeur, and Shelomi—had never seen me cry before that day. Most of my players hadn't either, except for those football moments that move you to tears.

"I'm not used to asking anybody for help," I said, my voice cracking. "I'm an independent man. Nobody understands. I want to do things for myself. But sometimes I just can't. And that's hard. That's HARD."

I had just spent twenty-three consecutive days in the hospital, having had nine surgeries. I had lost nearly forty pounds and had let a scruffy white beard take over the bottom half of my face. I was like a sunken shadow of myself.

At first I thought I was going to correct an old toe injury from my playing days that had caused me pain for nearly two decades.

Then it was all-out panic from my people: I got rushed in for a follow-up and the doctors said they weren't sure if I would MAKE IT OUT OF SURGERY ALIVE. I mean, it's about a month after the surgery that was supposed to get me out of the woods . . . and now they are saying THAT? Then it became possible they might have to amputate my leg. Or they might have to take my foot. None of these were good choices.

It would've been easy to say "Why me?"

Instead, I said, "Why NOT me?"

God chose me for this. God is good. God is using me for the good. God always gives the largest struggles to His strongest soldiers.

Let me ask you something. Is your life a complete mess? Are you burdened by an illness, financial problems, or important relationships that seem to be falling apart? Are you broken? The easy thing—the TYPICAL thing—would be to just give up. Surrender to the pain. Lean on some addictions. Blame it all on somebody else. Play the victim.

Don't you DARE do that!

You keep GOING. No matter what, you keep MOVING. I know you've heard this before, but life is not a sprint. It's a marathon. We go through seasons—darkness and light, darkness and light—and we are STRENGTHENED by adversity.

I'm extremely lucky. The surgery didn't kill me. They discovered I had femoral arterial blood clots—they run in my family—that made my anatomy look like I had been smoking for thirty years. The blood just wasn't getting to my foot. The doctors fixed that, but they had to amputate two toes—my big toe and my second toe—on my left foot.

Hey, I told them let's make a deal. Take my leg, take my foot, take my toes (they did), whatever. But DON'T TAKE MY LIFE. Yeah, looking back, I had a tough time, a horrific experience. You know what? I'm still moving. I'm still going. I'M STILL HIM.

I still plan on DOMINATING.

The enemy is trying to disrupt my MOBILITY. He's mistaking it for my ABILITY. He thinks if he stops my MOBILITY, he can stop my ABILITY. That's not true.

When I came out of the hospital my voice was gone. I could barely talk. The anesthesia and medication had taken a toll on me. I was completely depleted. Another trick of the enemy, because my communication skills are a tremendous gift. My ability to inspire, encourage, motivate, and articulate what I've seen is what I use to change lives. The enemy wanted to disable my biggest gift.

I was not discouraged by any of this. Because as long as I have a life, as long as I have a voice, I will DOMINATE. If I stop going, if I stop moving, if I get discouraged, he wins. And I promise you, I'm NOT going to let that happen. I had some physical setbacks, but I'm still going to WIN. The enemy came at me in a MIGHTY way. That tells me I'm destined to accomplish some MIGHTY things that he wants to stop.

But this time I needed help. I am still human. From time to time, my mind drifts and I have some depressing thoughts. I'm going to tell you something you probably never thought a guy like Coach Prime would EVER say.

Sometimes it's hard to find the words. Occasionally it flashes through my mind.

One day I'd like to run again.

Can you even imagine? Me not being able to run? Man, I used to be like the Road Runner. *Beep! Beep!* I was gone. Nobody was catching me, sprinting, high-stepping. I once ran a 4.1 in the 40. *A four-one!* All my life I'd been the fastest guy you'd ever meet. Yeah, sure, we've all got to slow down at some point.

But man . . .

Those first few months after surgery were the most troublesome time in my life. I prided myself on never needing anybody.

I'm still focused and locked in, trying to be strong for the kids. But for the first time in my life I couldn't get up unless I was being helped. I couldn't go to the toilet without assistance. They put up ramps at the entrance to my home so I could get in there with my wheelchair. Depending on others like that BOTHERED me so much.

I remember waking up from the toe amputation surgery and looking down at my foot for the first time. I was like, *Oh my God, I've never seen something like that before.* You think about what kind of athlete you are, then you see yourself in that state. It's very, very difficult.

I thought about my high-stepping and my dancing, the days when I did EVERYTHING off my mobility. Then I look down and think, *Oh, that's gone. So what am I going to do now? How am I going to do what I do?*

The shock is the recognition of the end of something, the recognition of the level of attack. It's like nothing you've ever seen before. You've got to process it for a minute, make your peace with it, then you're ready to resume the fight.

No question about it, I've been through one hell of a fight. But the blessing in all this is that I can share my experience and teach you based on this very difficult lesson I went through.

For a while I felt broken and sorry for myself. Then I snapped back into shape and went down the path we all need to follow when things seem rough. I knew that I just had to heal.

I was back coaching as soon as possible. My mind was never far from the game. Of course, there are days when I wish this never would've happened and I was completely healthy and able to sprint faster than some of my players. But that's not the reality. I'm doing ALL I CAN with WHAT I'VE GOT. I went through quite a battle, but I came out the other side.

Keep going. Keep moving. Don't surrender. No matter how bad you think it is, DON'T QUIT.

The Pain That Wouldn't Go Away

I know some of y'all saw the video of me in my electric wheelchair and my scooter. You probably read about my health concerns because it got big headlines in 2021 when they thought they needed to take my leg and in 2023 when my circulation pain just wouldn't go away.

How did it EVER get to that point?

I'm not positive—mostly because all football players are ALWAYS hurting physically—but I think my problems started when I played for the Dallas Cowboys. I remember one particular game against the Cardinals.

I broke on a pass route and I kind of stumbled. It felt like something heavy had landed on my left foot. I went to the sideline and said to myself, "Something's not right." But I went back into the game.

Well, the opposing coaches see everything from their top perch. They noticed I was kind of limping. So they went right at me with a slant, but I picked it off. And if I'd been able to run normally, I would have scored because I was at about the 20-yard line. I hopped down the sideline and nearly got to the end zone, but they knocked me out at about the 2.

At first they called my injury a turf toe—a severe sprain of your toes. But it was much WORSE than that. I remember going to a specialist in Carolina—the number one doctor—and he wasn't sure if I'd ever play again. It was THAT severe. Then I went to a doctor in New York who was famous for working on ballerinas to get them back up on pointe. He performed my first toe surgery. There was a tremendous process of getting back on the field, but it felt like it got right.

I had three toe surgeries while I was playing. And ever since I retired, my foot has always caused me pain. I could never walk pain-free. I could never walk barefoot. On my left foot, I always walked on my heel. It ALWAYS hurt.

But I wanted to stay in shape, so I would still run a mile a day. At Jackson State, after practice, I ran ten hundreds with my assistant coach, Jason Phillips. Then I got in the big round ice tub to soak my foot and try and dull the pain.

I had a hammertoe, where basically my second toe was sitting on top of my big toe. So, before my second season at Jackson State, in 2021, we decided to get surgery and straighten out that toe. They examined me, and one doctor said it seemed like my foot had been dislocated for close to fifteen years. No wonder it hurt so bad! I was grateful to FINALLY be going in to fix things and I was looking forward to some relief.

When I got back to practice after the surgery, it was still hurting. I thought it would eventually go away, but it was getting worse. I took cortisone shots on game days just so I could make it through—and that DEFINITELY was not the normal recovery for this type of surgery.

But you know, I'm a former football player. I'm a football coach. I don't have time for this kind of nonsense. I'm toughing it out. I took time to have the surgery, so I trusted that it was getting better.

Our trainer, Lauren Askevold, came in to change my bandages every day. Well, one time she looked down there and my toes were completely JET-BLACK. She had this shocked look on her face. Lauren said, "Coach, this is NOT normal. We've gotta get you to the hospital. I mean, RIGHT NOW."

I told her, "OK, Lauren, we'll go to the hospital. But I'm not going anywhere until we have our practice. I mean, this has been my life. I'm always in pain. That's been my life for YEARS. Let's get our practice in, then we can go to the doctor."

When we finally got to the hospital, the doctors hit the roof. My foot was BLACK and my toes were BLACK because they weren't getting any circulation. They found blood clots all up and down my leg, so I had to be rushed into emergency surgery. I wasn't aware of this at the time, but the doctors were all over the map. They weren't sure if I would make it. They thought they'd have to amputate my leg or maybe my foot.

I was still thinking about my football team. We got my coaching staff on a Zoom call and I pretty much laid it out. I said, "Guys, you know what I've been going through. What are we doing with my toe? OK, now it's blood clots and now we're talking about amputation."

Stone silence. Everyone frozen in place.

They put one of the doctors on the Zoom so he could explain everything that was happening and just how serious THIS was going to be. Given the nature of the situation, it might sound crazy to y'all, but we got most of our game plan in before they took me away.

It took them three different procedures where they tried to alleviate my blood clots. This was quickly turning into an ordeal, and my management team set up an office in the hospital. With each procedure, the outlook got a little better, and they determined that my leg could be saved. They spared my life, but they had to take a couple of my toes. And it was going to be a long road back.

That's as broken as I've ever been physically. But even as depressing as that was, as DESPERATE as that was, I knew I had to keep moving. I knew that God had spared me and that He had a plan for me. I was not done yet.

That's my lesson for EVERYONE: You never give up, no matter how bad it gets.

If your problem is about money, it's not a problem. You can get more money. If it's about health, that's different.

My biggest problem was missing some Jackson State games, which just about killed me, but there was nothing I could do. My hospital room overlooked our stadium. How crazy is that? I could only watch the games on TV. I couldn't even stay in communication with my coaches because that's an NCAA violation.

So just when things seemed to be stabilizing, just when we'd avoided the big amputation, I came down with what they call "compartment syndrome." That's when your legs fill up with fluid. Basically, they're going to burst. I was sedated, so I don't really remember most of this, but my team said they literally had to slice open the side of my leg—we're talking six inches, no small puncture—and they LEFT IT OPEN so the fluid could drain out and it wouldn't back up. It was insane.

My situation was dire, but I'm an ATHLETE. When God gives you life, you've got to make the most of it. I had plenty to live for and I had great incentive to make it back.

When I started to get better, I was able to get visitors. But in the outside world, nobody really knew what was going on or how serious this really was. My team would put something out on my social media every few days or so, but we kept it on the down low.

Being in the hospital that long, I was extremely vulnerable. But when my coaches checked in, even on my darkest days, I was as positive as I've ever been. I tried to pump them up. I told them I was "eight toes down," behind them all the way. Hey, no matter what's going on, you've got to laugh sometimes. They told me later that my spirit on those days gave them some extra juice.

Dramatic Finish

Most days I wasn't laughing too much. I had never missed one of my son's games. I mean, NEVER. I'm there in the hospital, fighting, withering away, and I'm seeing Shedeur's passing percentage going down each game. I knew he was struggling with it. He came in and said, "Daddy, I need you." Well, that was it. I was breaking out.

We were playing Southern University, and I was there on the sideline in my wheelchair, all frail in the freezing cold. But I wasn't missing it. If you're a parent, and your child says he needs you, you're breaking your neck to do whatever possible.

Shedeur brought us from behind. They were driving down, trying to go back ahead in the final minute, and Shilo picked it off. I looked at the scoreboard and realized we were going to win the game 21–17. We had twenty-one points—MY NUMBER! I was there to witness it and that moment meant EVERYTHING to me. Forget the Super Bowl or the World Series. That moment right there topped them all.

It took a long while before things seemed back to normal. I was on a Zoom call, and when I looked down I noticed that my foot was bleeding. On a break, I got Lauren to dress the wound to stop the bleeding. They had taken some skin grafts from my thigh to patch it up. But I was still on blood thinners, so if I started bleeding, it was very tough to stop. Before the Zooms started again, I met with my athletic director, Ashley Robinson, and looked down at my foot again. Now there's a PUDDLE of blood. It is bleeding PRO-FUSELY.

So Lauren goes, "We've got to get to the hospital right now." Sam Morini, a member of my management team, was driving, and they put me in the back seat, so they could prop up my foot with pillows. They were very careful because with every bump that car hit, there was excruciating pain.

Sam is usually a fast driver, but he was being very cautious because there were so many potholes. He knows we need to go quickly, but he doesn't want to cause me pain, so he says, "What version of my driving do you want? Fast? Slow?"

He's going slow and easy. So I tell him, "Dude, I'm bleeding out. You've got to punch it." I was trying to joke around, but this was not funny.

We finally got to the hospital, and they stopped the bleeding. Sam was able to drive me home, and believe it or not, the bleeding starts ALL OVER AGAIN. I lived out in the country, about forty-five minutes from campus, so we were far from the hospital, but we had to do something. We finally found this small urgent care in the middle of nowhere, so that was our only choice.

Remember, we still hadn't released the news to anyone about what was really going on. No one knew about the blood clots or the toe amputations. There were rumors going around, but most people didn't know what kind of procedure I had endured.

We told the medical staff, "Look, what you're about to see right now, no one knows. Be prepared for what you're about to see. And you can't be TELLING ANYONE!" They assured us about the HIPAA laws and they did their job. They got the bleeding to stop.

Things calmed down after that with another skin graft and more recovery. But you NEVER get completely used to a situation like the one I faced.

Of course, there were moments during my recovery when I felt helpless and hopeless. The recovery is a lot more mental and psychological than physical. But I tried not to let those feelings linger.

Do I wish I had my full mobility? Of course I do! God has challenged me for a reason. I keep fighting the fight, and sometimes I make it look easier than it really seems. I'm faced with a daily challenge and a new normal. When you're BUILT FOR SPEED and you can't do that anymore, you have no idea how much that hurts.

But there's only one choice: I've got to take care of myself and do the extra stuff so I can move around the way I do.

I don't know what you've got going on or what you're going through in your life. I know it's SOMETHING. It's always something. But you've got to promise me that you'll keep pushing, keep moving, and never give up.

We're all going through something. The key is to have faith and KEEP ON GOING!

Working Through a Crisis

Sometimes life is NOT easy. Believe me, I am FAMILIAR with that concept.

Life will get you down, kick you while you're already down, and make you feel like you're never going to make it. But here's the thing: You CAN'T stay down. You can't. And you won't.

You get back up, dust yourself off, and keep going. Period.

Look, I know it gets hard. Maybe you just got fired from your job. Maybe you lost someone you loved. Maybe you're battling an illness that nobody knows about. Maybe your dreams have been shattered into a million pieces.

Whatever it may be, know that you're not alone. I've been there. I've had my share of struggles and setbacks, but I can tell you that quitting is NEVER an option.

Keep pushing, keep grinding, and keep chasing your dreams. It WON'T be easy, but it WILL be worth it.

Some people say the strongest steel is forged in the hottest fire. That means when you're going through a tough time, that's when you're being tempered and strengthened. That pain won't last forever. It's there to make you GROW. To make you jump higher, run faster, and be better.

Now, don't get it twisted. On the days when you feel like throwing in the towel, when you feel like giving up, that's when you must dig DEEP. Sometimes you have to FAKE IT till you MAKE IT. Sometimes you have to put on your brave face, even if you feel like crying inside.

Just know that it's OK to feel broken and discouraged. It's OK to feel like you can't do it. It's OK to feel weak.

But never forget that you are STRONG, you are CAPABLE, and you are WORTHY. The key is to keep moving. Keep putting one foot in front of the other, even if it's baby steps.

Celebrate every little victory, every little step forward. Because that's what success is made of. It's not about the end result. It's about the journey. It's about the stories you'll tell your grandchildren one day.

So when life knocks you down, GET BACK UP! When you feel like you can't go on, take a deep breath and keep moving. When you feel like you're broken and discouraged, remember that you're not alone and YOU CAN DO THIS!

You got this.

You're a CHAMPION. AND CHAMPIONS NEVER GIVE UP.

We're All Going Through Something

How well do you know the people at your workplace? Pretty close to a lot of them, right? What if I told you some of them are going through an absolute tragedy and crisis RIGHT NOW? Even though they smile at you each day and make all the normal small talk.

Would that surprise you? It shouldn't.

That old saying is true. We're all going through something—every single one of us—even if you may not know about it. Some people are just good at hiding the CRAZINESS in their lives.

I can tell you from experience with a football team, there are always life struggles going on. I've seen it where it gets too much, where some guys need to step away from the game for a while to take care of their stuff. When you have a group of fifty-some players—it gets to be more than a hundred in college ball—life's problems creep in and you'll never have a time without issues. You just learn to deal with it.

They won't cancel the game unless it's something extreme. With all the injuries, football players are conditioned to a "next man up" mentality. Somebody goes down, the team keeps going. You plug somebody else in there and go.

You get a few games into a season and EVERYBODY has got something wrong with them. You just learn to play through it, unless it's something more serious. At your work, if somebody needs to go to the hospital or has a broken leg . . . that stuff is obvious and everybody can see that.

But what about the stuff we can't see? Everybody these days is living with some kind of pain, whether it's the pain of yesterday, the pain of something with your child, the pain of loss, or the pain of addiction. There's always pain.

I know dealing with that kind of pain may not be easy. But you've got to keep going, too. The thing that has changed for the better these days is people are more open about asking for help. And there are so many more resources. That's a good thing. Because we can't do this alone.

You know, life is funny sometimes. It can throw you a curveball when you least expect it. One minute you're cruising along. Everything is going great. And the next—BAM!—you're hit with a challenge that shakes everything up.

And sometimes it's hard to talk about those challenges. It's easier to withdraw, maybe flash a fake smile and keep your head down. But that's no way to live. People need each other. We need to TALK about our problems. We need to draw off the energy of our circle.

It's just human nature to feel like we need to put up a certain facade, like we pretend everything is OK, even when it's not. If you're checking out social media, it might seem like you're the ONLY ONE who's having life challenges. Not true at all. The reality is we're all hiding behind something. Being honest with your feelings and asking for help isn't something a lot of people feel comfortable with.

We're afraid of being judged or criticized, so we keep our struggles to ourselves. And that's the WORST thing you can do, because that's a crazy burden to carry. Here's the thing: We don't have to go through it alone. We don't have to feel ashamed. We're all human, and it's OK to not be OK.

It's so important to treat each other with compassion and show each other some RESPECT. You never know what somebody is going through on the inside—even if they're smiling on the outside.

I've been there, y'all. I've had my own struggles, my own battles to fight. And I know how hard it can be to ask for help or reach out to someone and say, "Hey, I'm going through something right now and I don't know how to deal with it."

But trust me, asking for help doesn't make you weak. It takes strength to admit you need help. So let's make a PROMISE to each other, right here, right now. Let's PROMISE to show each other compassion, to lift each other up, and support each other, no matter what. Because we're all going through something, whether it's big or small. We all need a little help sometimes.

Not a darn thing wrong with that.

Keep your head up, stay positive, and remember that we're all in this together.

Take Care of Yourself

No matter how bad it gets, no matter how many crazy challenges get thrown in your path, you have to keep going. And I know you will.

You must TAKE CARE of yourself, too.

These days there's so much talk about self-care and paying attention to your mental health. I know it's on everyone's radar. But what does that look like exactly? What can you do?

If you've got needs, you've got to be specific and let your people know. Write your needs down on note cards if that helps and refer to them when somebody asks what's up. Don't expect people to read your mind. Look, most people WANT to help, and they'll be glad to help, especially if you reach out in a sincere way.

There are some good self-help books and podcasts out there. Filling your mind with the right kind of thoughts will get you going. But since you've got my book in your hands right now, let me fill your head with the right kind of thoughts that will get you going.

You probably need some quiet time. And when you get that, there's no shame in giving yourself permission to reflect and maybe even grieve. If you keep pushing those feelings inside or act like they don't exist, it will catch up to you eventually. Be HONEST with yourself.

I've always felt that one of the best medicines around is SUNSHINE. To take the pressure off, get outside, let the rays roll all over you, and try some feel-good activity. That's all good for your physical health, too.

Remind yourself of the good things going on in your life. There's probably a lot more than you think. We tend to focus on the negative, and who's going to live a confident life if they're always harping on the bad stuff? Think POSITIVE!

If you have a mentor or somebody you really trust to bounce around some ideas with, bring them into the picture to talk it out.

I know you got it in you to overcome, and a lot of that is just showing up every day. Time does have a way of healing just about everything.

But it's also a process—sometimes a long process. Don't forget to take care of yourself as you keep up the fight. Give your body and mind the rest they deserve, so you can find the strength to keep on going.

COACH PRIME'S TAKEAWAYS

1. **When life knocks you down, get back up.** Determined people have a funny way of creating their own luck. If you keep showing up, no matter how tough it gets, you're going to come out on top.

2. **The strongest steel is forged in the hottest fire.** You're going to learn how to be tough and that will help you later. The pain of today won't last forever.

3. **Nobody's living a perfect life—forget about what you see on social media—so you're not the only one who's facing some problems.** Everybody has something going on, including you!

4. **Show each other compassion, lift each other up, and support each other.** The help you give could be the help you need one day.

5. **Take care of yourself physically and don't ignore your mental health.** Take breaks when you need them to recharge and don't hesitate to ask for some help.

CHAPTER 2

Set Your Own Thermostat

Your mornings are so important. That's when you set your thermostat for the rest of your day.

I'm particular when it comes to setting my home's thermostat. My body runs warm, so sometimes I'm sleeping with the thermostat set at 68 degrees. But when I get up, I don't want it freezing, especially if it's real cold outside. So I'll turn it up a bit. When I'm ready to leave the house, I'll head to the window, look outside, and turn the car on remotely so I can get the temperature just right because I want that drive-time atmosphere to be comfortable and conducive to some good thinking. With every move throughout life, I'm always evaluating the thermostats in my environments to make sure they're ideal. Maybe that's just me, but having that right setting makes all the difference.

Setting the thermostat for your day is more about setting yourself up for success. When I get up after a good night's sleep, I don't like noise. I don't like confusion. I don't like to be presented with the problems of the day first thing. I prefer to stay away from the nonsense in those first few minutes.

I want my peace. I want my joy. I want to decide what my word for the day is going to be—it just comes to me, whatever pops into my spirit—and I want to flush my mind out with my thoughts. By the time I'm up and around, I'm ready. I'm ready to go get it.

Setting your thermostat is about getting your mind right and deciding on the priorities for your day. It's about some quiet reflection before jumping into the craziness. It's about shedding the trivial details and not getting upset over things that don't really matter. It's about putting yourself in the right mode. Because it's not just about you. You're trying to inspire somebody in the morning. You're trying to help someone, touch somebody and bless somebody. It's not about what you're dealing with personally, but what you feel in your spirit that needs to be seen right now.

So just start the morning, one foot in front of the other. It's not about hitting the snooze button until you have just enough time to get to work. This is about starting your day the right way, getting up with a purpose. Some of y'all like to ease in, but a good way might also be hitting the gym or taking a brisk walk around the block, anything to get the blood flowing.

However you start your day, your engine needs some fuel. That means protein. And when you're chowing down, don't forget to hydrate. You've got to keep hydrating, even when you're not feeling thirsty.

Whatever number of accomplishments you get done or not done in a day can usually be based on how that day got started. If your thermostat is in a good place, that's a really good sign. When your eyes blink open, you're at the starting gate for your day. Trust me, you put in a good morning, you get stuff done and get your mind right, it's going to set the right tone for your whole day.

Sometimes your family structure might cause that thermostat to be altered. If you have kids who need to get going or a spouse who needs a little attention in the morning, you might need a new plan. But you also need to find that time for yourself, when you get yourself together and get ready for the fight. Because it's a fight every day, a multitude of challenges the world's throwing at you. That's OK. Nobody said it would be easy. And you wouldn't want it if it was. When you get your day started in the right way, you can RESPOND to those challenges.

Find a Good Routine

"We are what we repeatedly do. Excellence, then, is not an act, but a habit."

That well-known quote is from the twentieth-century writer Will Durant, who based it on something he read in the works of Aristotle, a Greek philosopher who lived before the birth of Christ.

Even back then, Aristotle was setting his own thermostat.

Even back then, most successful people were following routines.

I think a lot of people make the same mistake. The first thing they do is revisit yesterday. Folks need to stop replaying their lowlights from the PREVIOUS DAY. They're still mad over something that happened, something they can't fix. Or they're worried about something that's coming up tomorrow. *What can I do about it tomorrow?*

Listen to me, y'all. Yesterday is GONE. Tomorrow is not here yet. You need to think about the day you're actually in. DON'T MISS THAT DAY. If I concentrate on my day and get that day's stuff done, it's going to prepare me for tomorrow.

Just stay in the PRESENT and establish a good routine. Block all the other stuff out. If you don't, it will eat you alive. Trust me.

You think success is about talent? It's not. First and foremost, success is about DISCIPLINE. That's true whether you're running a business, leading a family, trying to pass your exams in school, or practicing your craft as a professional athlete. It's about showing up every day, putting in the work, and being committed to the process CONSISTENTLY.

And the only way to do that is to stay in the day you're in. You think you can fix something that happened LAST WEEK? You think WORRYING about the future is gonna make you more efficient?

All you can control is the MOMENT. That's why it's so important to have a great routine. Having that routine is like referring to a road map. It helps you stay on track. You feeling a little lost? Stick to your routine. That helps you take the steps necessary to achieve your goals.

Now, here's the deal about a routine: You better commit to it! You've got to BELIEVE what you're committing to. You can't skip days. You've gotta stick to it EVERY SINGLE DAY.

If you're telling me that you don't have time for a routine, I'm telling you that you better FIND TIME. There's ALWAYS time to prioritize the important things in your life. It must be at the top of your list. And don't think a routine is just about doing the same thing repeatedly. It's about being INTENTIONAL with your time and using it wisely.

Y'all ever hear that question about how you eat an elephant? That's right. One bite at a time. When you have obstacles that seem insurmountable and you don't feel like doing anything because you're overwhelmed, you just gotta START.

Any perfectionists out there? Y'all listen up. This is NOT about being perfect. It's about being consistent and consistently doing something to move forward. I like the quote "Well begun is half-done." That means stop overthinking it. Get off your butt and DO SOMETHING. Even if it's just a little thing, it'll get your juices flowing and you'll get more fired up about finishing. Because you're certainly not a quitter.

Oprah Winfrey's routine begins with opening her eyes and simply saying "Thank you." She is about having GRATITUDE. I love that. That's a good way of starting your day—with a smile on your face.

Either You're a Believer or a Belief

If you have a basic belief, setting your thermostat comes naturally. It's just part of who you are.

I am a BELIEVER.

When you say that, people automatically think you're talking about your belief in God, your belief in Jesus, your belief in the Bible. And with me, that's all true.

But here's what I believe:

Either you're a BELIEVER or you're a BELIEF. You have to figure out which one you really are.

OK, what's that all mean? I'll tell you right now.

When you're a BELIEVER, you are the creator of your own destiny. Whatever you believe, whatever you manifest, whatever you create—no matter your situation or background—if you fully believe it, you embody it and you BECOME it.

Whatever you BELIEVE, that's what you ARE.

Those are the elite folks, the leaders, the difference-makers.

But here's where most people fall short: They are stuck being a BELIEF.

What's a belief?

That's what your mama and daddy told you. That's what people have told you about yourself. That's the environment where you grew up, your circumstances and the things that have happened to you in life. You are now on this fence, this wall of beliefs, these things that have been PROJECTED onto you by society.

Only YOU can control or change what's inside that fence. Only YOU can change what you already believe about yourself and whether to believe what you've been told.

That's where people get stuck. Sometimes they can't move past what they've been told or the stereotypes that were given to them.

Do you think I was TOLD that I'd be playing in the NFL and

making millions of dollars? Do you think they PREDICTED I'd be playing in the big leagues? That I'd live in beautiful homes or be able to take care of my mama FOR LIFE or I'd be working in television?

Or that I'd be a major college football coach?

Or that I'd be writing a darn BOOK that could help people?

Nope. I heard none of that. What I did hear was "Well, you can only do this much. This is all you'll ever be. You can't go much further than this. This is what society has for you."

That was the BELIEF that was put on me. It would've been easy to just act like that. But I wanted a change. I became a BELIEVER.

NOBODY was gonna decide who I really was—except me.

Don't believe all the lies that are told about you. Don't believe all the talk that you're stuck where you are and there's nothing you can do to change it. It just isn't true.

You are WORTHY. You deserve the BEST. Now you're going to face adversity and it all won't be perfect. The way to beat it is developing the mindset that YOU are in charge of your life, and YOU are determining your life's path.

So that's what you must do. Become a BELIEVER. That way, YOU get to decide who you really are. And that way, you can keep that thermostat in the same place every day. It doesn't matter what's going on outside your doors or what somebody is telling you. When your thermostat is on that same setting, your life is in a very good place. You're in control.

Feeding Your Mind

Just like it's important to fuel your body in the proper way, it's also vital to feed your mind.

Is that music for relaxation? Is that a great book for inspiration?

Is that listening to a podcast for some good perspective? Is that taking out your journal and writing down ten new ideas? Is that soaking up some knowledge and learning more about the things you'll be doing that day? Is that meditating?

It might be ALL of the above. All those things are great techniques to trigger your mind and put it in a productive place.

When I was a kid, I thought being fed in the morning meant a bowl of breakfast cereal. I didn't know it also meant I could set up my own pregame show with my mind and plan the best way to tackle the day ahead.

Let's break this down:

Reading is like mental exercise for the brain. As I've gotten older, I've realized what a pleasure it is to be exposed to so many ideas. I love to improve my vocabulary and concentration. When I come to a word I'm not familiar with I'll repeat it and try to find a way to use it in a sentence. I want to OWN that word. You can get that mental exercise with books, newspapers, and magazines. Now you can LISTEN to the books and the articles, maybe when you're driving, so I'd also encourage that.

I can't believe how many podcasts are out there and the range of subjects they cover. Whether you're into sports, politics, history, entertainment, or anything in between, there's one for you. It's a great way to keep up with the news and what people are talking about. I'm always learning something. And sometimes it's just a way to get a good laugh in at the start of my day.

Journaling is a cool way to help you get your thoughts down on paper. It can also be therapeutic when it comes to working through anxiety or stress. Now, you don't have to be a professional writer to make this work. I promise you on that one. Just jot down a few thoughts or goals for the day. It will help you feel more focused and motivated.

What if you just need some quiet time? What if you don't feel like putting forth a great mental effort? That's when meditation helps you like nothing else. How does it work? Just breathe. I'm SERIOUS. Just find a quiet place where you can be alone and breathe in and out. Focus on the moment you're in. Get all that hurry and stress out of your life. Just be. If you get in a few minutes of quiet reflection, I'm telling you, it makes all the difference to your day.

OK, I saved this one for last—music!

Here we go, y'all. Can you imagine life without music? Can you imagine not having that feeling when you hear that song you absolutely LOVE? New music opens your mind to different forms of expression. Old music reminds you of a wonderful time in your life and somebody special from your past.

Music can make you calm. It can get you pumped up. It might put you in an upbeat frame of mind. Music has the power to affect our emotions and moods in a powerful way. So put on your tunes and let the rhythm move you. Or just use it in the background to keep things happy and light. Music can do all those things.

When we play our theme song for the day prior to kickoff in the Colorado locker room, it just brings us together. It's not that deep, but it's very effective. We're all on the same beat with the same chords as we move together to our song. It's unifying. And it's usually something that just . . . HAPPENS. It's not planned out. Music has no color, no shade. It transcends all ethnicities. It's beautiful in the way it brings people together.

You get your mind and your mood just right, and you can ATTACK that day. And that's just what we're after here. We all know the mind is an incredibly powerful tool. So we need to feed it just right, and keep it in good shape.

Whether you have good thoughts or bad thoughts, those mental images become your reality. If you keep feeding your mind with the good stuff, there's no limit to what you can do. And you know what? Instead of dreading the morning, you might start liking it.

COACH PRIME'S TAKEAWAYS

1. **The morning is when you set the temperature for your day.** So learn how to set your own thermostat. Put yourself in a POSITION TO WIN from the beginning by fueling your body and feeding your mind.

2. **You should establish a good morning ROUTINE.** Now, it won't be that easy. I'm talking about DISCIPLINE, y'all. You have to be INTENTIONAL with your time. Does it seem too hard? Set yourself some goals, then break them up into manageable tasks. You won't change the world OVERNIGHT. But if you're making some progress in the right direction, you're good.

3. **This one is REALLY important. Either you're a BELIEVER or you're a BELIEF.** When you're a believer, you're the creator of your destiny. There's nothing you can't accomplish. When you're a belief, that's what people say, what society projects on you. It's the stereotypes some people can never escape. To reach your potential, you need to be a BELIEVER.

4. **Don't buy into all those false thoughts and crazy mental images that run through your mind.** If you're not careful, they become your reality. Whether it's through music, reading, podcasts, or journaling, you gotta fill your head with positive thoughts and possibilities instead of dwelling on your doubts.

5. **To jump-start any morning, you've got to DO SOME-THING.** Any forward movement will give you positive momentum and end inertia, so make that a priority. Remember, well begun is half-done. Or like the old saying goes, the smallest deed is greater than the grandest intention. You need to dream. But at some point, you've got to DO!

CHAPTER 3

Be Where Your Feet Are

We are all incredibly busy. Between family, relationships, jobs, hobbies, and downtime, we're always jumping from place to place. For many people, it feels like they're always running fifteen minutes behind the next thing they're scheduled to do.

Let me give you some advice.

Slow down.

Take a breath.

Be present.

Be where your feet are.

Look, I get it. We all want to be great at EVERYTHING—great parents, great spouses, great workers, great friends, great students—all of that and more. And most of that is very achievable. But we must be careful and mindful of our priorities.

I love this Bible verse:

Ecclesiastes 9:10—Whatever your hand finds to do, do it with all your might, for in the realm of the dead, where you are going, there is neither working nor planning nor knowledge nor wisdom.

And here's how I translate that: Put your best effort into EVERYTHING you do. But most of the stuff we prioritize, most of the stuff we think is SO DARN IMPORTANT, should AL-WAYS take a back seat to family and relationships. Like we hear all the time, nobody is on their deathbed wishing they had spent more time in the office.

Can we ignore our work? Can we step aside from the business of life? No, we can't. But we can design our days where those things are in their proper place and they don't infringe on what's REALLY important.

Here's how I like to say it:

When you're at work, be at work.

When you're at home, be at home.

Don't get those two confused. When you're home playing with your kids or spending time with your spouse, don't obsess over some project waiting for you on your desk. When you're locked in at work, don't be worrying about some inconsequential thing your kids did yesterday or something your spouse expects you to do on the weekend.

I'm a good one to study when it comes to being where your feet are. Remember, I played professional football AND major-league baseball. Sometimes they collided. And I had one occasion where I suited up for BOTH on the same day.

How did I keep that straight? When I played football, I never allowed anyone to talk baseball with me. When I played baseball, I never allowed anyone to talk football with me. During the NFL season, I wasn't thinking about hitting the curveball. During the MLB season, I wasn't thinking about covering Jerry Rice or Michael Irvin.

You have to set priorities. Setting those priorities should be part of your daily life, but it's VITAL to know that you can't be in two places at the same time. If you try to do that, your task at hand will not be getting its full attention and it's going to suffer. And you don't want anything to suffer in life.

When Bruce Arians was head coach of the NFL's Tampa Bay

Buccaneers, he set the tone for a healthy work-life balance with his coaches at their first meeting.

"For our coaches, I tell them, if you miss a recital or a football game or a basketball game, I'll fire you," he said. "You can always come back and work. Those kids are not going to be there forever. They're going to grow up and be gone."

Arians and the Bucs, by the way, won Super Bowl LV.

Arians said he developed his philosophy from his experience as an assistant with the Kansas City Chiefs, when Marty Schottenheimer had a strict policy on his assistants ALWAYS being present in the office. In order to see his son's games, Arians told everyone he was going jogging and snuck away. On the way back to the office, he threw some water on his face so it looked like he was covered in sweat.

Look, I'm not asking you to cheat on your job. But you don't want to cheat on your family either.

When it's time to be a parent, be a parent.

When it's time to work, do your work.

If Bruce Arians can have his priorities straight at the highest pinnacle of sports—winning a Super Bowl, while he and his coaches are present for all their important family activities—why can't we ALL live that way?

When Michelle Obama was first lady, before she booked any kind of meeting or conference, she sat down with her assistant and looked at her life. On the schedule, she filled in her family time obligations first—potluck dinners, date nights, workouts, vacations, sports activities, and summer downtime. THEN . . . she put in her work.

Why did she do it that way?

She said we all have a "problem with the corporate culture." Everyone is conditioned to let work inundate EVERYTHING in their lives. Work, work, work . . . then fit the other stuff in somewhere . . . maybe.

Just imagine a different way of doing things. Why not put your life BEFORE your work? When you schedule your family first, trust me, there's still plenty of time for work. Why can't we see it that way?

Time for a change, y'all.

Keep your priorities straight.

Get your work done, but don't let it override your family life.

And always be where your feet are.

Plan Your Time, Time Your Plan

Most of us don't try to plan our life. We just live it. You hear people saying, "I'm just going with the flow," like that's a good thing. Hey, sometimes it is. There's a place for flexibility. You don't want to be too rigid. But for the most part, that old cliché is so true.

If you fail to plan, you plan to fail.

My little twist on that statement is this:

Plan your time and time your plan.

If you live your life by accident, if you are unaware of how to prioritize your tasks on a given day, you will NOT be in a perfect position to take advantage of opportunities. Point blank, planning your day is the key to success. That's how you take advantage of being where your feet are. If you don't know what you're doing, how are you going to get anywhere? I've always been a planner and it truly has helped me achieve everything I've ever set my mind to.

Here's a suggestion.

The night before, you need to find some quiet time. That's when you think about your next day and how it's going to unfold. Start by writing down your goals for the day. Or maybe text them to yourself. Then break those goals down into smaller steps. Once you have a plan, you can start working on it one step at a time.

When I played in the NFL, I studied my practice script. I VISU-ALIZED what I wanted to accomplish. I VISUALIZED having success. This is a very powerful tool and helps to train your subconscious mind. Basically, you are experiencing a situation that hasn't happened yet as if it's real.

I use the same technique now as a head coach. The practice plan sets the tone. Everybody is on the same page and we don't let anything interfere with our schedule. We are completely locked in until that final horn goes off.

But before we achieve our success, I need to see it in my mind.

Visualization is so important. Did you know that when the actor Jim Carrey was first starting out he constantly visualized himself as rich, famous, and successful, even when he had . . . NOTHING? He used to drive around Los Angeles and pretend he was meeting with directors—and no one even knew who Jim Carrey was. He did this for himself. People might have thought he was crazy, but he could see the goal as clear as day.

Sounds like he was living in a dream world, right? But he tricked his mind and told himself all of his dreams were out there waiting for him. They were going to be his actual possessions. He just didn't have ahold of them yet. It was going to take time.

When he was broke, he made out a check to himself for $10 million. He was convinced the money would come his way one day in the future. He dated it Thanksgiving 1995 and tucked it away in his wallet. Just before Thanksgiving Day 1995, Carrey learned he was going to make ten million for a film called *Dumb and Dumber*. Jim Carrey kept that check in his wallet until the day he buried his father, putting it inside his father's casket because together they had had the dream of him making it.

Visualization is powerful, man. It's one of the highest forms of BELIEF.

When Jennifer Lopez went from being a backup dancer to a singer to an actress, her biggest goal was to star in a romantic comedy. That might not sound like such a crazy dream these days, but back then JLo looked at all the rom-coms and saw white women as the stars. She was from the Bronx, a Latina. No woman who looked like her was EVER cast as the star. Well, as you probably know, JLo has been the star of MANY successful romantic comedies, which she not only starred in but also went on to co-produce. She VISUALIZED herself in those movies . . . years before they came out.

She had BELIEF.

Now let's translate that belief to your situation. One of the biggest ways to make your belief a reality is through constant preparation.

When I was a broadcaster, I didn't just show up and start talking. I planned my interviews in advance. I did some research on who I was talking with so I could ask the right questions. I didn't want to waste anybody's time, and everybody always appreciates it when they know you have properly prepared.

You know a funny thing about broadcasting in general? Did you know that some news broadcasters are required to plan out their wardrobe almost A YEAR IN ADVANCE? I'm totally serious. You're sitting there in January. You look at April 10 and you already know what outfit you'll be wearing that day, so you won't show up wearing something similar to what another broadcaster is wearing.

How many of you have been at your closet in the morning and said, "Oh my gosh, what am I going to wear today?" The advance planning of the wardrobe eliminates any potential for time-wasting, and it's about as efficient a system as I've ever seen. Even in high school I laid out the outfit I was gonna wear the night before. I ironed it, too.

Now, I know some of you think that sounds ridiculous and anal. But let me ask you: Is it better to have no plan, waste your time, and get nothing accomplished?

There are ALWAYS positives that occur when you plan out your time, then time your plan. If you're going to be where your feet are—and not living in two worlds at the same time—you've got to account for your activities to maximize your potential.

Let's summarize.

Here are some tips I can recommend to help plan your day:

- **Set some clear goals**—What do you want to accomplish?

- **Break them down**—Make your goals into smaller, more manageable tasks.

- **Prioritize your tasks**—What needs to be done first?

- **Schedule**—Arrange your tasks in a way that makes sense.

- **Leave time for flexibility**—Things don't always go according to plan.

- **Take breaks throughout the day**—Don't try to do everything at once.

- **Reward yourself**—When you accomplish something, why not go for the treat?

Avoiding the Parent Trap

Planning out your days and being efficient with your work schedule allows you to address one of the most important issues of being an adult—spending time with your family.

You don't want to be absent. And you don't want to be THAT PARENT who's home playing with the kids but your mind is elsewhere. Put your darn phone down! Stick it in an old shoe, then wrap it up in a towel and stick it in the closet. That phone is what leads to distraction and not being present. We used to live just fine without those phones, and now we're letting them rule our lives.

I believe in family. I believe in raising your kids. I believe in tucking them in at night. It's important to me for our team to get its work done early enough in the day so that our coaches can get home and take care of their family responsibilities.

Get your butt home. Have dinner with your family. Get to your kids' games, practices, recitals, competitions, and plays whenever possible. Ask about their lives. Read them a story. Do something silly and make them laugh. Then get your butt up the next morning and do it all over again.

All of this can be accomplished with a plan. It takes some re-focusing and maybe cleaning off your binoculars. Because if you really want a marriage, you stick to your plan. If you really want to be present in your kids' lives, you stick to your plan.

I know you feel the pressure of finances. You think you can never stop working because you have to provide for your family. But I guarantee you those kids would rather have dedicated time with you instead of anything you might buy them.

When you're at home, you need to be at home. Being where your feet are becomes a profound statement that really allows you to be your best self. You don't want to be distracted at work. And you don't want to be impatient and snapping at your kids because of some frustrations back at the office.

When a person is stressed as they try to live in two worlds, you can hear it in their voice and see it on their face. It's hard to hide because they become a little more irritated, a little quicker to anger, a little more antsy, and they don't have their full attention on the details. Your kids are going to sense this.

Let me give you some fatherly advice. As a parent, you don't ever have to be perfect—and you never will be perfect. But you do have to be PRESENT.

You need to be that role model for your children—not some model playing a role. Be involved in their life and share your values because they are looking up to you. Be a role model they can reach out and touch because kids are always looking to grasp on to something. Be a positive force in their life.

It's not the easiest thing, being in the spotlight and being there for your children the way they need you to be. You know who's a tremendous father? LeBron James. Just outstanding. Denzel Washington is also a solid father and an example of a good man. I think Master P is an excellent dad, and I really respect what he did in cleaning up his hip-hop music to set a better example for his children and kids in general.

Trust me, I know there can be some obstacles with the relationship you want to build with your children. I've been divorced twice. A few years ago, three coaches on my staff were going through divorces.

Sometimes you need to coach your coaches—and not just in football. You want to make sure everybody has their priorities straight. They're trying to get to the next level, but you sit down and have some good life talks with them. You try to give them situations and analogies that hampered you, so they can learn from it and do better.

The biggest thing I want to sell them on is being present for their kids. To be great at something you MUST be there. You have to be like-minded and intentional. Nowhere is that more important than with family.

My oldest kids, Deiondra and Bucky, never lived full-time with me, mostly staying with their mom. But I always took them to school on certain days and had special activities with them, time that we shared together, regularly. I helped to coach their teams so

I could stay close with them. I can also recall taking a helicopter from one side of town to the other just to be on time for their games. For me, it was always about being present in their lives.

Even today I want to do that with each of my five kids. Sometimes we all do things together, but they also really like separate time with their daddy.

Being a father to my three sons and two daughters means the world to me. And so does being accessible to my kids. I want them to feel like they can talk to me about anything and everything. And I feel like we have that kind of relationship.

Probably like y'all, I feel like my kids have grown up in the blink of an eye. You get to the point where you loosen up on your expectations, meaning you want them to live their own lives instead of imposing your plans on them. You give them roots, which keeps them grounded and safe, and then you give them wings.

It's a lot of stages, but the biggest thing is to always remain present in their lives. When you stay where your feet are early in your kids' lives, you're setting yourself up for a lifelong relationship that's going to bring the joy and happiness you always dreamed of.

Winning the Day

Most of us are dying and we aren't living.

Let me say that again.

Most of us are DYING and we aren't LIVING.

I'm not talking about somebody with an illness or a disease. I'm talking about somebody who is 100 percent healthy. But they're just going through the motions of life. They aren't productive. They don't have a plan. They aren't even close to reaching their potential. They're dying. Those people look around and they're upset with the person who is actually LIVING. They're jealous. They want to be living, but it's almost like they don't know how.

I'm going to show you how.

Now, we're always going to be where our feet are, right? We've got that part down. And we're going to be planning, making sure we're ready for the next day with the right priorities and visualizing our success. OK, we've got those parts down, too.

Then it's all about WINNING THE DAY.

I am a planner, but I'm not so far down the street that I lose sight of the task at hand. I know where my feet are, so I'm going to DOMINATE THE NOW. You've got to look ahead in planning, but I'm never so occupied with tomorrow that I'm missing today.

How do you win your day? It's all about the attention to details and the passion for your purpose.

I'm convinced that if you want to be great, you must be detail-oriented. I've seen so many people with all the talent in the world never reach their full potential because they can't grasp the importance of details.

People see the big plays and touchdowns. But football players live in a world where their stance, their footwork, and their hand placement make all the difference.

Once you realize the importance of details, you should make a conscious effort to notice the little things. If you're organized— or you learn a system that will help you stay organized—you're going to stay on top of things and avoid making careless mistakes. By being meticulous, you'll make sure everything is done correctly and you'll have pride in your work.

That's the small picture.

But there's a big-picture angle to this, too.

Why are you doing what you do? Why is it important to you? That's your purpose, the thing that's fueled by passion.

Passion is what drives us. It gets you out of bed in the morning. It gets you excited about the next day. It's the thing that makes us the best we can be.

Passion will keep you motivated because you're more likely to stick with it—even when things get difficult. It will make you more creative because you'll always come up with new ideas and solutions to achieve your purpose. It's going to make you happier. When you're that passionate about ANYTHING, it's going to bring more joy and fulfillment into your life.

When you do those things, your entire existence is going to be more productive and peaceful. You'll be living, not dying. Most importantly, you're going to win the day!

COACH PRIME'S TAKEAWAYS

1. **Put your best effort into EVERYTHING you do and concentrate on the task at hand.** Don't ignore your work. But don't let your work override everything else in your life. Prioritize your family and relationships. Trust me, there will be plenty of time to get that work done.

2. **Have a plan for your day so you don't waste any opportunities.** Things happen, so you can be flexible and change the plan. But the important thing is having that plan.

3. **Visualization is one of the most powerful forms of belief.** Plan out your successes and see them happen in your mind before they become a reality.

4. **If you have kids, be PRESENT in their lives.** Participate in their activities. Get to know their hopes and dreams. Don't show up to be with them and have your mind elsewhere. Your kids will ALWAYS remember that you were there for them.

5. **Once you know how to be where your feet are, your biggest task is WINNING YOUR DAY.** That's all about your attention to detail and the passion for your purpose. If you stay focused in those areas, you're going to DOMINATE THE NOW.

CHAPTER 4

Make Confidence Your Natural Odor

I don't use cologne. Somebody might pick up on my scent and ask, "What is that you're wearing?" I just say, "Confidence."

Confidence is my natural odor.

And you need to make confidence your natural odor, too.

Some people call it arrogance or cockiness. I've always referred to it as CONFIDENCE. Nothing wrong with being confident. Nothing wrong with believing in yourself. And I don't think there's anything wrong with verbalizing that belief.

You know how sometimes another person will enter the room and they just seem DIFFERENT? They look you dead in the eye and shake your hand. They speak well. They dress nice and feel right at home in the conversation. They are comfortable. They are CONFIDENT.

That's who you want to be.

I don't care if you're giving a presentation in the boardroom, making a sale to a customer, giving a persuasive speech to your class, or laying down the law for your kids. You don't want to be hemming and hawing in those situations. The way you present yourself, the way you sound, and the way you carry yourself means everything.

You want to be CONFIDENT and project it.

I learned early on that I had to believe in myself. Because

who's gonna believe in me if I don't? You need to have that same aura at your work. You need to know that there's NOBODY more qualified to do your job than you. You are the expert and you're going to KILL IT every day. That's the attitude you need as part of your personality.

Some people might be uncomfortable if you present yourself this way.

Here's what I tell them: "Don't allow my CONFIDENCE to OFFEND your insecurity."

I need to repeat that one:

"Don't allow my CONFIDENCE to OFFEND your insecurity."

If you are EDUCATED and PREPARED and SINCERE, if you truly have an interest in people and you have total COMMITMENT and BELIEF in what you bring to this world, then you are going to be naturally CONFIDENT. And there's not a darn thing wrong with that.

Performance Breeds Confidence

Now, we all know lots of people who talk the talk but don't walk the walk. They talk a big game, but don't deliver.

PERFORMANCE is how you know if somebody's confidence is justified. I don't care what you do for a living, the greatest job security in the world is performance. If you know your business and you care about doing a good job for people, you're always going to perform. So that's the foundation for your confidence—and that's a SOLID foundation.

Before you get drafted into the NFL as a rookie, they take you to the combine. It's like a huge speed-dating session for football players. They're looking at you, measuring and weighing you, asking all kinds of questions about your past and your history. It's supposed to be where they see how strong you are, how fast you are, and whether you pass all their tests.

In my mind, the only reason I needed to be there was to run the 40-yard dash, so I could show them I was who I was. That I really was THAT FAST.

Well, little did I know that they had me signed up for the bench press. I was engaged in conversation with one of my cohorts, and over at the bench press they kept calling out, "Sanders! Sanders! Sanders, get up here! It's your time to do the bench press."

I looked at them and said, "No, I don't think Jerry Rice is gonna lay across my hands and have me bench press him, so that's not necessary. I'm good."

When it came time for the 40, I did WHAT I DO. And that was run fast. I ran it and I killed it. It was time for me to show the world and I did. I kept on going and I left the building. I KNEW what time it was because I had prepared for it. There was nothing more to talk about.

I don't think that's ARROGANCE. To me, that's beautiful CONFIDENCE.

You know your job, right? Nobody knows it better than you. Stop feeling like you got to be all modest all the time. Sooner or later you've got to bet on YOU. You don't have to look back and see how many hand claps you got. You already know. You should always bet on yourself. You believe in everybody else, right? You're propping up your friends, telling them they're worthy. You support them. You're baking cakes and making cookies for everybody else.

But when are you going to look in the mirror and start pumping up the accomplished person that you really are? You've got to believe in YOU. Because you got it. You got it. Now SHOW IT to everybody. Show the world. That's all I've ever done—show the world the person that I know I am.

At that NFL combine, after I crossed that finish line, I didn't even look back and ask what my 40 time was. I didn't have to. That's my life. Those are my skills. I KNOW what I'm all about. I know my training and preparation and knowledge. I live it every day.

You don't have to look back and see what your sales are. You don't have to look back and see what your engagements are. You don't have to look back and see how effective you are.

You already know.

You should always bet on yourself.

I'm not a gambler. I don't play with money of that nature. When I go to casinos, which is rarely, they don't even give me free rooms because they know I'm not going to spend any money. But every now and then, I will go to the roulette table and put some money on 21 Black. That's just an analogy, just a symbol of me always believing in who I am.

Now, here are my last words on performance. I'm not perfect. I'm not a perfect father. Neither am I a perfect man. I always tell my kids that. But when they look around, I'm going to be there at every turn to support them and love them. I put in the work.

So, if you know your business, if you're putting in the work, that's really all you need. Most of the people you deal with are a little uncertain. They have some doubts. They're holding back. If you bet on yourself and come out CONFIDENT, you're going to stand out.

You're going to win. And when you win, it's okay to do your dance.

Be Who You Say You Are

Here's an interesting experiment for y'all. Why don't you gather up some coworkers and family members and ask them about your most recognizable qualities. What kind of person do they think you are? In their eyes, who do you PROFESS to be?

Then ask yourself a question.

Are you that person?

We all do a lot of talking these days, whether it's in person or on social media. We have an IMAGE or a PERSONA to the people who know us best.

Sometimes, you'll hear a comment like "Wow, that kind of behavior was really out of character for my friend." So, there are normal expectations for who you are, what you represent, how you're going to react to everyday things. That pretty much represents who you say you are.

It's easy to be a good person when people are watching. But it's a whole different thing to be a good person—to be WHO YOU SAY YOU ARE—when no one is around. That's when your true character is revealed.

I am VERY familiar with the spotlight, and I am a household name. People know me—and recognize me—most places I go. My challenge is always being the same person, with the same values and principles, no matter who is watching.

Y'all got a platform, too. If you're the boss, if you're a key performer in your business, certainly if you're a parent, you've got other people watching you ALL THE TIME. You parents already know the importance of having and keeping a consistent message. You start switching that up and your kids are going to get really confused. They'll darn sure call you on it.

So what are the best ways you can be who you say you are when no one is looking?

> **Be kind**—Even when you're having a bad day, be kind to the people around you. It doesn't take much. A smile and a kind word can make a huge difference in someone's day. You know what? Make sure to be kind to YOURSELF, too. When you're driving hard toward your goal, there's a tendency to put pressure on yourself—maybe too much pressure. Give yourself a break. Treating yourself well is always important.

- **Be honest**—Always tell the truth—period. Even when it's hard, don't misrepresent yourself and don't exaggerate things. We're all human, and sometimes it seems easier to play fast and loose with the truth. Here's the truth—lying will only make you feel bad in the long run.

- **Be forgiving**—Everybody makes mistakes. If somebody does you wrong, as tempting as it might be to rub it in, you need to forgive them. Holding on to anger and resentment will never serve you well. At times, that means forgiving YOURSELF, whether it's for a silly mistake or something that keeps haunting you from the past.

- **Be respectful**—Treat EVERYONE with respect. The way you treat the CEO should be the same way you treat the cleaning crew. Things like age, race, religion, and social status don't matter. If you treat human beings like human beings—and you do that every day—you will solve so many problems.

I'm sure you want to be viewed as a good person, someone who is honest and dependable, someone your people can count on. EARN that reputation. Be who you say you are.

Humble Yourself

This one might surprise you: A big part of being who you say you are—and living a confident life—is being able to HUMBLE yourself.

Yes, you can be CONFIDENT and HUMBLE at the same time.

Humility is a virtue that is really overlooked, particularly in the world we're living in, where everybody seems to be chasing attention.

You can't get caught up in worshipping your social media followers and the comments you attract. It takes away your focus and it just isn't real.

When you're humble, you're not afraid to admit that you're wrong. You're not boastful about your accomplishments. And you're always willing to help other people.

Being humble doesn't mean that your confidence has been diminished. It just means that you don't let that confidence go to your head. That you aren't letting insecurity get the best of you. You know you're not perfect. You're always willing to learn and grow.

Here's the real benefit to being humble: It makes you more likable. People are drawn to the people they can relate to. And if people are drawn to you, what does that mean? They're going to believe in you and listen to you. That gives you a leg up in your business.

It takes a lot of self-awareness and discipline to admit when you're wrong and to give credit to others. But that also makes you more open to feedback and advice, which helps you improve your skills.

Confidence in yourself also gives you confidence in others. There's no need for you to hog all the credit. None of us can get places without the help of others. Always recognize the contributions of others and don't take any of those blessings for granted. Be sure to express thanks to those who helped you along the way.

I'm confident in the gifts God has blessed me with, but I'm also grateful for the people He placed around me. And I never want to forget where I came from. The first thing you see me do every morning in my office is clean things up a bit, maybe even vacuum the hallway. That makes me recall who I am and what I am. I'm NOT too good to clean up. The way I see things, I can't ask a custodian to pick up a piece of paper on the ground if I'm not willing to do that myself.

That custodian is a person just like me. What's the difference in some people's eyes? It's probably that I have the title—Head Football Coach—and they do not. So what? It's a darn problem if you start thinking your TITLE is who you really are. A title doesn't justify you. It just locates you.

It's disgusting when someone with a high title becomes arrogant and condescending, like they believe they're better than everyone else. It's like they're living in a bubble, and they don't understand the struggles of others. It really gets bad when these people become corrupt and use their power for personal gain. They stop caring about the people they're supposed to be serving.

Having a title or a high position should be a VERY GOOD thing. Your position can be used to make a positive difference in the world. Your platform can raise awareness of important issues and be used for resources to help those in need. It should never be used for personal gain.

I like to think I can show people it's possible to achieve great things, even if you come from humble beginnings. I sure didn't come from wealth or privilege, but I did have a dream and a lot of desire. If you have a similar story, use THAT to inspire others to be their best selves. And you can show those people the importance of being kind, compassionate, and helpful, even while achieving your professional goals.

Little Things Mean A Lot

The attention always goes to the big things, right? You get a BIG promotion. You close the BIG sale. Your company lands a BIG account. Your child gets accepted to a BIG college. It's easy to be confident in moments like that. It's also easy to get carried away with those achievements because they are special and worthy of a celebration.

But let's be real, y'all.

None of it ever happens if we don't concentrate on the LIT-TLE THINGS, the fundamentals, the stuff that hardly ever gets any attention.

I'm a firm believer in doing the little things well. Over time, if you focus on doing your best at the so-called inglorious tasks, it's going to add up to much more significant things. And when you're on that big stage, your CONFIDENCE will be well founded because you have earned your accomplishment and you've worked your way up in the right manner.

You don't want to be one of those all-show, no-go types of people. Others will pick up on that quickly. At the same time, they're going to immediately sense the truth if you're one of those people who do things correctly.

What are some little things that could make a big difference for you?

- **Arrive EARLY for appointments**—It shows you're punctual, organized, and respectful of someone else's time. If you're made to wait, bring along a book to read or write in your journal. Make use of the extra time.

- **Be POLITE to everyone**—Even people you don't know. ESPECIALLY people you don't know. If you're a "yes sir" and "yes ma'am" kind of person, if you hold the door for others, if you're especially courteous to people who serve you in stores or restaurants, others will notice that you have a lot of class. Be respectful, regardless of someone's outward appearance.

- **Take care of your BODY**—If you eat healthy foods, exercise regularly, and get enough sleep, it's going to come across in the way you look and the way you feel. You'll ALWAYS feel on top of your game.

○ **LEARN something new every day**—Whether you read books, watch educational videos, take online courses, or attend conferences and workshops that relate to your business, you're going to make yourself better, not only for now but in the long run.

○ **GIVE something back**—Do this by volunteering in your community or donating to a worthy cause. Not only will you be helping others but you'll feel a lot better about yourself while building a reputation that others will notice. Learn to give without the expectation of reciprocation.

The little things mean a lot.

COACH PRIME'S TAKEAWAYS

1. **Confidence means everything, y'all.** Learn how to make confidence your natural odor, the unmistakable scent that's part of your everyday life. To achieve this, be prepared like crazy, have a sincere interest in people, and be totally committed to excellence in your family and business life. All of this will give you NATURAL confidence.

2. **Your consistent performance is always going to be your best job security.** Do what you do. And do it to the best of your ability. That's going to be the foundation for your confidence. When you rely on your preparation and knowledge, it's always easy to bet on yourself.

3. **Be who you say you are.** Nobody likes a fake person. Be authentic. Be unapologetically YOU. Never have those moments where friends say, "Wow, that's really out of character for you. I didn't expect that." Make your actions match your reputation.

4. **Is it even possible to be CONFIDENT and HUMBLE at the same time? Yes, it is!** Humility shows you're an actual human and it's going to attract people. If you're likable, self-aware, and disciplined, those aspects of humility actually display quiet confidence. Mark my words: People will practically line up to do business with you.

5. **Little things mean a lot.** No matter how far you go in business and life, never forget where you came from.

And I'm not necessarily talking about your hometown. Never get away from the fundamentals. Behind every big-time achievement or accomplishment there's usually a person who's punctual, polite, studious, and meaningfully involved with their family and in their community. Most overnight success stories involve people who have spent decades doing the little things properly.

CHAPTER 5

Are You a Leader or a Dog?

Just because you're at the head of the line and getting stuff done, that doesn't make you a leader.

Just because you talk real loud and get people's attention, that doesn't make you a leader.

Just because everybody's clapping for you, that doesn't make you a leader.

There's no shame in not being a leader. Instead, maybe you're a dog.

Now, let me explain this because the word "dog" gets a bad rap. Like if somebody performs poorly, they're called a "dog," or people say an athlete's "dogging it."

The meaning has changed. Today, a dog is somebody who takes control and takes command of the situation. They don't wait. They act. They GO GET IT. They subdue and dominate.

ON MY TEAMS, WE HAVE LEADERS AND DOGS.

And we need them BOTH, whether it's in the workforce, a family, or a football team.

YOU KNOW WHAT I LOOK FOR IN A LEADER? Usually, the qualities are very subtle. That person is going to assess the situation, clearly state the objective, and get everyone moving in the right direction. They're going to be definitive and decisive.

When they walk into the room, you WILL know they're in charge. And without question, they're going to know where to find the dogs.

Leaders make decisions.

They won't take it to the committee, then hem and haw and waste time and ask everybody, "Well, what do you think?" Don't get me wrong. They ask questions. They listen. But when it's time for the decision, they ACT.

And they don't look back. If things don't go well, they wear it and don't make excuses. If that decision turns out great, they don't take all the credit.

People know who the leaders are, and the leaders don't need a letter on their chest to prove it.

Let me give you a football example. Captains are usually a big deal in sports. In fact, some athletes are known as "the captain." I just feel like the word "captain" should be reserved for the military or police. I feel strongly about that word. And as a result, I don't have captains on my team.

EVERY LEADER ISN'T A DOG. AND FOR DARN SURE, EVERY DOG ISN'T A LEADER.

Dogs are killers. They get things done and serve as the backbone of any good organization. They're tenacious. You turn them loose on something, they're relentless. They do not hesitate and they are workhorses.

Dogs execute the plan. They have a work ethic like no other. And they always finish the job because their pride would never allow anything else.

Even though leaders and dogs have different skill sets, they are similar in one very important way. They are both DECISIVE. Whether it's making a tough call or producing at crunch time, you need a get-it-done mentality.

So, which are you? A leader or a dog?

It doesn't really matter because we need them both. But now I'm going to show you how to operate like an elite leader. And you top dogs out there will appreciate that.

It's possible to be the new person in an organization and put yourself in position to become a leader. Some people just have those natural skills and instincts. But listen good to what we're going to tell you about effective leadership, which basically means your folks will listen to you, believe in you, and carry out your plans.

The best leaders are usually great listeners.

The Leader's Mindset

First, let me ask you about your work. Even if you're the boss right now, you probably once worked for someone or reported to a supervisor. If I asked what you loved the most about your FAVORITE boss, I can almost GUARANTEE your answer.

"With that boss, we didn't have to guess about anything. We ALWAYS knew where we stood."

Am I right?

The best leaders are great communicators. They explain the plan in detail. They "hand the plan" by giving you those details in written form, maybe in an email, so you can commit it to memory. They go over it again, fine-tuning it in real time, adjusting if necessary.

You don't have to guess. You just follow the plan. And that leader is going to be there for follow-up.

Y'all ever had leaders who you hardly ever SAW? From what I can tell, this happens a lot. The boss never leaves their office and keeps the door closed most of the time. There's an aura of unapproachability, maybe even a little fear, definitely a lot of uncertainty. Half the time, you have no idea what this boss even wants or what they're thinking. What the heck is going on behind that closed door, anyway?

That is NOT the way to be an efficient leader.

To be the right kind of leader, there are four key strategies to keep your folks engaged and motivated:

Keep them INFORMED.
Keep them INVOLVED.
Keep them INTERESTED.
Keep them INSPIRED.

And every single one of these factors revolves around COMMUNICATION.

You know the top reasons why people leave their jobs? You might guess they're going with another company that's paying them more and giving them a chance to move up. Sure, that's part of it everywhere. You can't fault somebody for getting a higher salary or a better opportunity. Happens all the time.

I'm talking about people who really DON'T want to leave their job, but they feel like they HAVE to leave. There were surveys done on this workplace phenomenon. You want to know their top reasons for leaving?

They need more of a CHALLENGE.
They're feeling UNINSPIRED.
They want to feel VALUED.
They need more FEEDBACK or STRUCTURE.

NOT ONE of those things is about making more money. But you know what? You could argue that ALL those reasons reflect a LACK of leadership. Sounds to me like these working folks didn't have much communication with their boss. Maybe they NEVER had an opportunity to explain their situations or what they needed.

Shoot, those bosses might have been SHOCKED when those folks left. *My gosh, I didn't know they were looking for another job. I thought they were HAPPY here.* That just shows you the disconnect that can exist when leaders don't communicate.

Start the Conversation

I've got a confession to make. I'm not great with names. But I'm REALLY GOOD with giving out nicknames because I can recall the player or colleague based on their mannerisms, their look, or whatever.

As a leader, you need to know your folks beyond the office. Who's in their family? What do they care about? How do they like to have fun? What are their long-term goals? If you know these things about your folks, you're going to have a great feel for how they're wound and how they're driven. That leads to INSIGHT and that's going to help you make better decisions when it comes to this individual.

Now, you might say, "What does that stuff have to do with getting the job done day-to-day?" It has EVERYTHING to do with it. If you have a motivated worker who feels like you've always got their back—and if you know the right buttons to push when things get tough—that mutual trust will give you the foundation that's essential for success.

With my football team, I want to know those athletes beyond the playing field, maybe becoming familiar with some intimate things about these kids. Sometimes I'll tell a few of them to come by the office. They aren't in trouble. I make that clear. But I just want to talk, about anything, really. I'll ask them, "What do you think about the crib you're living in?" And that will bring us a form of connectivity because they'll start to open up.

I started having sessions with many of our players who had tremendous potential, not the ones who were problematic, but the ones who I felt needed focus and solutions. They're showing ability, but they need help. I feel like if I don't get to them, they'll either remain stuck or misguide others. Most of the time, they're great kids who just need love and attention. I can tell this in a heartbeat, just by watching the way they interact with their teammates and how they're playing.

Well, I had this one player, a left guard, who was a good kid with a lot of personal stuff going on. I had no idea what it was, but you could tell he was suffering, and it was affecting his play. So I had him come to my office for a session.

I always empty myself first. I told him about the period of my life when I was suicidal, all my trials and tribulations. That cleared the air and allowed him to feel more comfortable sharing what was maybe going on in his life.

What came out was his girlfriend had cheated on him and broke his heart. He was in love. It troubled him.

I kept it real with him. "Dawg, the thought process that you're going to marry her is really slim. That does not happen anymore, having a girl in high school and taking it all the way through. She's not the only girl out there. And she's certainly not the only girl for you. I know you're going to find a great girl and a beautiful one. Are you kidding me? I guar-an-tee you it's going to happen. You are THE MAN."

He started smiling and laughing. It was like a big weight was lifted from his shoulders. I could see him changing right there in front of me. He needed to unburden himself. This kid is picking it up, picking it up, picking it up . . . and then he starts dominating. He's got all his swag going on. He went on to become a FIRST TEAM ALL-CONFERENCE PLAYER!

He made that happen. But it wasn't until I started talking to him that things began to change. I was giving him love and understanding, just meeting him at that point of contact. If I had never had that session—if I had said I was too busy after practice and not opened up to him—that kid might not have turned it around during the season.

Hear me out: If you're a leader, you must COMMUNICATE with your people. ALL YOUR PEOPLE.

Be Clear with Your Expectations

As a leader it's your job to set the tone for your team. You need to let them know what you expect from them, whether it's their work, behavior, or the company culture.

If you're not clear with those expectations, your team will be LOST. They won't know exactly what you want, and they'll be more likely to make mistakes.

When you're communicating those expectations, be CLEAR and CONCISE. Don't beat around the bush. Be direct and to the point.

And don't just tell them what you expect. SHOW them. Lead by example. If you want your team to be hardworking and dedicated, YOU need to be hardworking and dedicated yourself. If you want your team to be respectful and professional, YOU need to be respectful and professional yourself.

Your team is watching you. They're learning from you all the time. So make sure you're setting a good example.

When you make those expectations crystal clear, the work environment is going to be so much more PRODUCTIVE and POSITIVE. Your team will not only know what they need to do—they'll be more likely to DO IT.

That means you're going to hit your goals. And isn't that the POINT?

Here's what I'm talking about:

Let's say you're a manager of a restaurant. Of course, you want your servers to be friendly and helpful to the customers, right? So, you're probably going to say something like "I expect my servers to be friendly and helpful. They should greet customers with a smile, make sure they have everything they need, and be polite and efficient."

Or let's say you're a teacher. You want your students to be respectful and engaged in class. So, you could say something like "I expect my students to be respectful and engaged. They should raise their hands to speak, listen attentively, and participate in class discussions."

Those statements are CLEAR and CONCISE. Kind of hard to misinterpret those expectations.

Now let's say you're not clear with expectations. You might say something like "I want my servers to be good." What does that even mean? What does "good" mean to you?

See what I'm saying? That's a way to LOSE your team and have them wondering just what they're supposed to do.

Leaders need to establish themselves early—with clear expectations. That's going to set the tone right there.

Holding People Accountable

Once leaders set those expectations, it's not the time to go away and hide or sit behind the desk with your feet up to watch some TV. No, no. Here comes one of the most important parts, where the best leaders always separate themselves.

LEADERS MUST HOLD THEIR PEOPLE ACCOUNTABLE FOR THEIR ACTIONS. If you don't, it's a recipe for

DISASTER. It sends the message that you don't care about the results, which slowly creates a culture of MEDIOCRITY.

Is that what you want?

Didn't think so.

When you hold people accountable, you're not just setting them up for success. You're also showing them that you believe in them. You're telling them that you know they can do BETTER . . . and that YOU ARE WILLING to help them get there. You aren't going anywhere until this thing gets right.

Now, how can you hold people accountable? There are a few ways. You can have a one-on-one conversation with them. You can call them out in front of the team. You can give them a written warning. In extreme cases, you may even have to fire them.

What's the best way? It depends on the situation. The most important thing—BY FAR—is to be CONSISTENT. If you let people get away with something one time, they're going to think they can get away with it again.

Do not BE AFRAID to hold people accountable. That's really the only way to create a high-performing team.

Here are some examples of how it can happen:

Let's say you have a team member who is always LATE for work. You could have a one-on-one conversation with them and explain that their tardiness is really affecting the entire team. Or you could set a deadline for them to be on time for work. And if they don't meet the deadline, you could take disciplinary action.

Let's say you have a team member who is always making mistakes. A one-on-one conversation could point out that their mistakes are costing the company money. You could set up a system of checks and balances to help them catch their mistakes before they become a much BIGGER problem.

These aren't the easiest things to enforce, because some people may push back or feel threatened. But as long as you're CONSISTENT, you're setting the right tone not only for them but for the entire team.

Here are a few quick tips on how you deliver the message:

- **Be specific about what you expect**—Don't just say "I expect you to do better." Tell them exactly what you want them to do differently.

- **Be fair**—Don't hold people accountable for things that are out of their control.

- **Be consistent**—Don't let people get away with things one time and then hold them accountable for the same thing later.

- **Be respectful**—Even when you're holding someone accountable, you should ALWAYS treat them with respect and professionalism.

The bottom line is that you're showing your team members you BELIEVE in them. If your message is delivered CLEARLY and CONSISTENTLY, they will understand that. And in time they'll greatly appreciate it, too.

Taking the Ultimate Responsibility

As the leader, your biggest job is making sure the team is successful. Therefore you must take responsibility for your actions. And when it comes right down to it, you've got to make some tough decisions.

If you don't step up and DON'T take responsibility, it's going to send the message that you're not in control and it's going to create a culture of blame. When you take responsibility, the team will pick up on your confidence and they will know that you believe in them. You're also showing that you're WILLING to take risks and you're NOT AFRAID to fail.

When it's on your shoulders, you've got to do these things and you've got to do them quickly. Admit when you're wrong. Apologize for the mistakes. Be honest and up-front. If you cover up your mistakes, the team will lose trust in you.

I take full responsibility if my team loses a football game. I might have made some coaching mistakes in the heat of battle. You never want to be in that spot, but you've got to be honest with your players and tell them you'll do better next time. The most important learning tool with mistakes is not repeating them and learning the lesson to get better.

All leaders know that at some point it's going to be up to them to chart the right course and make a tough decision—hopefully, the right decision. Sometimes, there are no easy answers.

So how do you move forward in the difficult moments?

- **Get all the information you can**—The more information you have, the better equipped you'll be to make a good decision.

- **Consider all the options**—There's usually more than one way to solve a problem.

- **Weigh the pros and cons of each option**—Consider the potential benefits and drawbacks of each option. What can you live with? What's off the table?

- **Make a decision and stick to it**—Once you've made a decision, don't second-guess yourself. And don't expect 100 percent acceptance. Everybody in a leadership position can tell you that half the crowd is usually doubting them.

People want to know that their leaders are confident and decisive. When it comes time for the tough decision, show the team that you're in charge and you're putting them in the best possible position.

COACH PRIME'S TAKEAWAYS

1. **Leaders make DECISIONS.** They don't rely on some committee. They aren't WISHY-WASHY. They gather the information they need. They consider the options. Then they ACT. There's no doubt about who's in charge.

2. **Communication is EVERYTHING.** No two ways about that. People leave their jobs because they want more money and a higher position elsewhere, but most of the time it's because they're not getting enough direction and they don't feel valued.

3. **Be CLEAR and CONCISE with the expectations that you set as a leader.** Don't just TELL them. SHOW them. Your people need to know that you truly CARE about them doing a good job.

4. **You must consistently hold people ACCOUNTABLE for your expectations of them.** If you don't do that—or if you don't do it well—it sends a message that you really don't care about good results. Over time, that creates a culture of MEDIOCRITY.

5. **You can't shrink as a leader.** Stand up TALL. You must take the ultimate responsibility and sometimes that means making the tough decision. Don't take those moments lightly, but don't run from them either. People want to know that their leaders are CONFIDENT and DECISIVE.

CHAPTER 6

Mastering the Three W's
(Want! Work! Win!)

L et's make this simple. If I'm your coach, if I'm your teacher, the
goal is for you to learn the lessons, right? We've already gone
through some techniques in this book, a lot of examples, a lot of
action plans that require strategies and execution. I know you have
soaked up a lot of different ways to reach your goals.

Now I want you to follow me into the grade-school classroom.
I wish this lesson was accompanied by music, so we could make it
into a little jingle. Yeah, it's kind of catchy. And I think it's the formula y'all should follow to achieve almost anything.

Here we go.

Let's do the three W's:

Want!
Work!
Win!

Those are your building blocks. That's your road map to get
wherever you want in life.

Want!
Work!
Win!

I don't care if it's a new truck, a new job, a new house, a five-course meal, your dream vacation, or peace on earth. If it's truly your heart's desire, you've got to *want* it.

Your boss can't want it for you. Your coach can't want it for you. Your family or friends can't want it for you. You must want it for YOURSELF. You've got to feel it deep down in your gut and make it a priority.

Now that you've got the goal in mind, you've got to *work* for it.

That's a little different from the want. Nobody's going to do it for you. You're probably not just going to fall into it. You've got to do the work. When it comes to work, life has a scoreboard that doesn't lie.

Consistency counts. Persistence counts. Determination counts.

If you do the work, you will have the opportunity to *win*. Let's not get this confused. We are put on this earth to win. It's very specific in sports, where winning means accomplishing your goals. It means coming in first. You can't fall short of the gold and say "I'm a winner!"

In other walks of life, there are different types of winning. But I'm a coach. There are two choices—elevation or termination. You might think that's cold, but it's the truth. There's no in-between. I prefer elevation because that leads to one of my favorite words— DOMINATION.

Want!
Work!
Win!

Here's what that formula has meant for me the last few years.

When the opportunity of college football became real, I had to make up my mind. Do I really *want* this? I definitely did. The ability to stay in the game that meant so much to me—and even greater, positively influencing the lives of young people—was the kind of challenge that really got my excitement going.

Then I had to *work*. You get your staff together. You recruit the players. You set up your practice schedule, surround yourself with elite people, get ramped up with the right facilities, prepare with the right scouting and strategy, and here we go.

You get all that working and it's time to win. It's the reason we've put all this together, the reason we put in the work. We HAVE to win. Because if we don't win, all the work is in vain. Nobody's going to feel sorry for you. The daily grind is real and you're fighting every single day to stay on top of this game.

Want!
Work!
Win!

That's what the formula means in my professional life.
What's it going to mean for you?

You've Got to Want It

When you identify what you're after, it's no time to be passive. You've got to want it. Everybody around you should pick up on that desire.

I believe that desire is the most important ingredient to achieving success. If you don't have a burning desire to achieve your goals, then you're not going to put in the hard work and dedication it takes to succeed.

But desire itself is NOT enough. You also need a WANT, that

thing you truly believe in, something you're willing to make sacrifices for. When you have a true want, you're not afraid to take risks and go after your dreams. You aren't fazed by the possibility of failure.

Abraham Lincoln once said, "My great concern is not whether you have failed, but whether you are content with your failure."

I had both desire and want when I was a kid, when I wanted to become a professional football player. I truly believed I could be great. That's why I worked hard, never gave up, and eventually achieved my goal.

How can you make YOUR want work for you?

I've always loved the idea of VISUALIZING myself achieving a goal. Some folks call that living in a fantasy world, but I believe visualization can lead to reality. If you start sensing what it looks like, what it feels like, those vivid details are going to fuel your desire and your want to get there.

When the Colorado job first landed on my radar, after some careful investigation, I knew we could turn that team around, win some games, and shock the world. I saw it in my mind—plain as day. When I said I was coming, so many people thought I was crazy. Why would I go to a 1–11 team that had been down for so long? Why didn't I take a job in the South?

This whole thing was CLEAR in my mind, even though nobody else believed. When I said we were gonna win, it wasn't boasting. I could SEE it. I could FEEL it. I can see around the corner now. It's a level of faith and belief that's difficult to articulate. But once you SEE it in your mind, BELIEVING is the easy part.

Did you know that Beyoncé keeps a photograph of an Academy Award by her treadmill, where she sees it every day? She is manifesting an eventual Oscar, that she will no doubt earn because of the work she does to get there.

Lindsey Vonn, the World Cup and Olympic gold medal–

winning skier, says she runs the race in her head about a hundred times before reaching the starting gate, including practicing her breathing patterns and picturing how she's going to make each turn.

Visualization keeps the dream alive, but so does an action plan. It helps to set SMART goals—and that's an acronym for Specific, Measurable, Achievable, Relevant, and Timely goals. The SMART system, which was originated in 1981 by George T. Doran, a former director of corporate planning for Washington Water Power Company, gets you thinking and helps to crystallize what you're really shooting for with your want.

Here's how to get there:

Specific—Here's where you lay out the target you're trying to hit.

Measurable—You've got to have a way to quantify your progress. Or as they say in the modern corporate world, "Let's see some metrics on this."

Achievable—Look at your resources. Look at your timeline. Be ambitious, but make sure this goal is within your reach.

Realistic—Put together an outline that shows how your goal can be achieved.

Timely—Come up with a deadline. You need an endgame.

Then you need to surround yourself with the right kind of people who understand your mindset. The people you spend time with can make a huge impact on your motivation. Getting positive reinforcement from them—along with leaning on a mentor or role model—can provide the needed confidence.

Life is hard enough, so ditch any negative folks who bring you down. Focus on relationships with people who give you positive vibes. And listen closely to this one: You NEVER want to be the smartest person in the room, even if that builds up your ego. That limits your ability to learn. Associating with people who are SMARTER than you and people who have deeper experiences gives you the ability to grow.

Identify and work to cultivate relationships with people who already have accomplished YOUR goals. They know what it takes. Pick their brains. Learn from them. Successful people are AL-WAYS willing to share their tips and tricks, so take advantage of that.

OK, you want it, right? You really, really want it? Let's take the next step.

Time to work.

You've Got to Work for It

Let me be 100 with you on this VERY important topic.

If you don't put the work in, you WILL NOT make it in life. Notice that I didn't say MIGHT NOT. I said WILL NOT.

Some of you understand work, so you just work. There's no need for any motivation. Some of you have to be pushed and encouraged to work.

I'll tell you what gets me really concerned. On my football team I have some players who won't make it because they don't embrace work—even though football is something they CHOSE to do. What happens when they enter something they really don't want to do, maybe some job that isn't optimal? How are they going to get where they need to go? How quickly will they just surrender?

To live the life you really want, you have to work for it. It's that simple.

Notice that I didn't say you have to ENJOY the work. I really wish EVERYONE had a passion for what they do. Like the old saying goes, if you enjoy what you do, you'll never work a day in your life. I LOVE what I do and ENJOY everything about the process, even the mundane details, so I'm very fortunate.

But even if you consider your work just a means to an end—a way to earn a buck, maybe purchase some high-end toys to bring spice into your life, or just continue supporting your family with a comfortable lifestyle—make sure you have an attitude that will keep your mind fresh and eager.

Always remain confident in your abilities. Take some pride in knowing you can get the job done and people are relying on you. If you speak up and share your ideas—instead of keeping to yourself and sulking—your colleagues will respect that.

Let your work ethic speak volumes. The world is full of people who cut corners and take shortcuts. Do things the right way and you'll always have a reputation for being a valuable member of the team.

I don't care if it's the worst situation imaginable. Don't let that affect your ability to be positive and professional. Look for the good in every position and be that person who's willing to help. Don't get caught up in office politics and the toxicity of complaining. Instead, show respect and support for your colleagues and your boss.

The world is changing. The odds are strong that your profession is changing, too. You'll get left behind if you continue to do things the way they've always been done. Be willing to learn. Keep up with technology. If you don't know something, ask. By adapting and growing, you'll show that you're willing to put in the effort.

The biggest thing is having the self-discipline to know the right habits, so you won't have to constantly get directed or corrected. You have to fight that tendency to procrastinate and learn to work through stressful situations. You must know the tasks that will have the greatest impact on your organization instead of putting all your time into lower-priority assignments or the things you feel are the easiest to accomplish.

The best way to learn how to work effectively is to watch the people around you who are successful.

If you're looking to get into better shape, when you go to the gym, find the people who have the best fitness levels. Ask about their workout routines and their diet.

Athletes can be copycats. They'll watch elite-level teammates and mimic their approach. Usually, it's about getting there early, staying late, and studying volumes of information. There isn't much of a secret formula.

One of the most legendary work ethics I ever heard about was Teddy Roosevelt's. This early twentieth-century president was an American cowboy. With a combination of strength and vitality, he seemed like he couldn't be stopped.

Teddy Roosevelt also meticulously scheduled his life. He made time for studying and all his extracurricular activities because he did the opposite of juggling multiple tasks. He believed in "deep work," which was focusing on ONE THING with your full effort.

"I never won anything without hard labor, the exercise of my best judgment, careful planning and working long in advance," he said.

There are examples of high-achieving people at all levels of politics, business, entertainment, and sports. So, if you want to build a better work ethic, study the people who get the work done.

When you identify the people in our society who are deemed

"winners," then dig deep into their backgrounds. You always find a common thread.

They were all ferocious workers.

Winning Is the Final Result

If you *want* it badly enough, if you *work* hard enough to get it, you're going to *win*.

So how do you define "winning"?

Great question.

With lots of different answers.

Of course, in the sports arena or in the business world, it's black and white. It means winning the game. It's about finishing number one. Like Ricky Bobby said in *Talladega Nights*, "If you ain't first, you're last."

What is a win? It depends on the circumstances.

Sometimes when I'm in my office, the custodian comes by to do her thing. I thank her for her work, sometimes giving her a hug or a high five. I tell her how much she means to this program. I tell her what a great job she does. I want her to know that the work she does counts. That she makes a difference. I feel that in this moment God is using me to validate her. And that's a win. A huge one.

When it comes to our football team, the most tangible form of winning is looking at our first game on the schedule and declaring victory if we have more points than the other team. That's definitely a win.

But the winning starts so much earlier with our off-season conditioning, spring ball, individual work, and summer practices. Winning starts with the attitude you have on Day One, when no one is in the stands cheering. The opening game is just where we allow the people to see what we've been working on for months and months. If you're a great team, the winning starts at the beginning, and it happens daily.

Don't overlook the small wins. They equate to big wins. Small wins place you on a stage where you don't get flustered, where you don't get sensitive or scared when the lights come on, where you are totally prepared when it's time to win big.

We're focused on winning from the first day a young person walks through the doors of our football program. I tell them that everything they get, they're going to need to earn. We establish our navigational system for their life. Then we talk to their mama. We have to make Mama feel secure that we've got her baby and we're going to make sure he gets a degree. And we're going to get him multiple opportunities on and off the field because the odds are against him playing professional football, but we're going to help him become a professional in some respectable field. We're going to show him love, respect, and honor—and we're going to teach him how to show those qualities to others as well. We're looking to shape future fathers, future political figures, future doctors, future lawyers, future teachers, and future community leaders.

That's winning.

The way you live your life can represent winning. I want to be a great father and a great human being, but you don't just wake up, snap your fingers, and have those things occur. You've got to work to make them happen.

I think about my grandmother, who has passed away. She never knew how to drive. But she got everywhere she wanted to go—and it wasn't because she was popular or notable. I never heard her use profanity. She won because she was never out of character. She won because every Sunday and Wednesday she was in Bible study at church. She won because she helped everybody she could and she was always so well loved.

In my mind, she's one of the ultimate winners.

Everybody loves to win. I'm a little bit of a different cat. I love the PROCESS. I love every bit of it, including the drudgery of preparation, because I know how it all feeds into the final product.

If you're looking for the shortcut or the fast-food approach, I've got some difficult news for you. There's no easy way to win in life. Following the process leads to meaningful things that last forever. Anything short of that and you're going to ultimately be disappointed. So, my biggest piece of advice is DON'T CHEAT THE PROCESS.

COACH PRIME'S TAKEAWAYS

1. **You've got to really WANT it.** You've got to WORK for it. If you go about the process the right way, you've put yourself in position to WIN.

2. **Visualizing what you want keeps the DREAM alive, but ultimately you need an action PLAN** and you need to surround yourself with supportive, positive people who will help nurture your dream.

3. **If you don't want to work, you will not make it in life.** Working can give you the kind of life you want. Having a great work ethic and self-discipline will be your ticket to accomplishing the biggest GOALS.

4. **There's all sorts of WAYS TO WIN. Small wins can equate to big victories.** You must treat the grind and the moments of drudgery along the way with the same respect as the moments when the lights are on and you're competing on the big stage.

5. **Don't look for a shortcut.** The process is clear. Want! Work! Win! DON'T CHEAT THE PROCESS.

CHAPTER 7

Know Who You Are
(And Who's on Your Team)

W*ho am I?*

Deion Luwynn Sanders Sr.

Born August 9, 1967, in Fort Myers, Florida.

Who am I?

All-American cornerback from Florida State University. Jim Thorpe Award winner. College Football Hall of Famer.

Who am I?

Fifth pick in the 1989 NFL Draft. The guy who revolutionized playing defensive back. Student of the game. The first athlete to play in two professional leagues on the same day.

Who am I?

Pro Football Hall of Famer. Television commentator. Entrepreneur. College football coach.

Who am I?

Man of God. Father. Mentor. Coach Prime.

I don't have arguments with any of those descriptions. Those are TRUE FACTS. You can look them up.

But that's the basic stuff. I have a standard bio and so do you. Those true facts, though, only scratch the surface of . . . *Who . . . I . . . Am.*

Now who are *you*? Who are you REALLY? That's what we need to find out. That's where we need to get.

Here's the thing. There are a multitude of people of all ages who are just lost. They're walking aimlessly through life, just trying to find themselves. Then they get attached to someone else who tells them who they are and who they should be—instead of figuring out WHO THEY REALLY ARE.

You've got to really identify who you are, what you are, why you're in that place, what you hope to be YOURSELF. Most people DON'T KNOW the true answers to these questions. It takes work and reflection to know the answers to these questions. HOW are you going to DOMINATE life when you don't know WHO YOU ARE?

Don't Buy into Preconceived Notions

As someone who is in their fifties, I've thought long and hard on things. I know me, I know who I am, and I've been through some things. I know what makes me happy, what makes me sad, what makes me angry, what gets on my nerves. I've experienced unexpected losses and the losses I expected. I've witnessed loyal friends, fake friends, and all kinds of backstabbing. I've seen family members pulling together and relationships get torn apart.

Nothing is going to surprise me about how I react to anything. And that's because I know ME. I know WHO I AM.

Sometimes, people get a preconceived notion of who they think you are and it's false. A character or quality they want to project, but don't really possess. You see it all the time in sports. Shannon Sharpe, the broadcaster and one of the best tight ends to ever do it in the NFL, is a dear friend. I always knew what he had in him. But it wasn't until he left CBS, where everything was a fifteen-second highlight clip, that America figured it out. Hey, this guy is smart. This guy is intelligent. This guy is really, really funny. A lot of people never knew these things, but he finally got the platform to expound on who he really was.

I think the same thing happened with me. Most of the country saw me on a football show, talking sports, talking about SOMEBODY ELSE while they ran the fifteen-second highlight clips. I gave my expertise on the situation, but that never allowed the public to know ME.

Over the last few years, when I became a college coach, I think the country has gotten to know me in a much more realistic way—as a steward of my players, a man of God, A FATHER, a leader. I've known this stuff for a while. Y'all are just getting to know me.

But all along, I knew WHO I WAS. And no matter what's going on in my life, I must be TRUE to that.

I'm going to be consistent with how I am. I'm going to be comfortable with it because there's nothing fake. It's who I am—24/7.

What I need to do sometimes—when I come across somebody in life that we're going to touch and elevate—is pull up a mirror. We've got to make people look in that mirror and examine themselves. If they're HONEST, they might say, "Dang, he's right. I need to change that or work on that."

Now, human nature being what it is, most people aren't going to pull up that mirror and be brutally honest with themselves. They aren't going to tell you about their transgressions or the deep goals they may have. It's EASIER and SAFER to hide inside a costume.

You can't be scared to find out who you are. Because the end goal for all of us—and I do mean ALL OF US—is to live our best life, our authentic life, every darn day. Seeing who we really are allows us to change the things we may not like about ourselves. But we can't do that if we aren't willing to truly see ourselves.

Sometimes, in the case of celebrities, people think the acquisition of money can change a person. I'm not sure if that's completely true. Money is only going to amplify the weaknesses and shortcomings we have. Money doesn't cover those things. It doesn't shield us from those things. I've always said money makes you MORE of who you really are. If you're broke and have an affection for alcohol, that means if you get rich, you're probably going to be a drunk. If you're broke with a bad attitude, that probably means you're going to be an ignorant rich person.

You ask me what I do for a living, and I'm telling you I'm in the PEOPLE BUSINESS. I'm successful because I'm constantly building a team of people who are SMART, TOUGH, FAST, DISCIPLINED with CHARACTER, and who embrace these values. I've got to pick the RIGHT ONES or my team won't be good enough. So I've got to look beyond the costumes.

And that's what you need to do, too.

Here's How to Build Your Team

I really don't know ANYONE who's extremely successful who doesn't have a tremendous team around them, a group of like-minded people who offer support and advice, the folks who become the strong point when we're feeling doubtful and weak. When you have people on your team who build a relationship of respect, you'll be able to tell each other intimate things that truly happened. They will listen. They will act. You get love and respect, and they'll always have your back.

But you don't have to be a CEO, head coach, or Jerry Jones to have a team. EVERYONE should have a team. And it doesn't have to be big. Sometimes a team can just be one or two key trusted people in your life who will both give it to you straight and be there for you to lean on while you get ready to go back out and do battle.

So, how do you find your team?

Finding the right people for your team starts with a continual self-audit. Examine yourself in the mirror. Figure out who you are and who you aren't. Then look at your friend group, the people who are around you all the time. Who's building you up? Who's bringing you down?

The people in your circle, they're either adding to you or subtracting from you. Maybe they're helping to multiply your blessings. Or maybe they're dividing you from things that are really important. To get the results you want in the MATHEMATICS OF LIFE, you've got to surround yourself with the right kind of folks.

I didn't get a lot of that support when I was growing up. My biological father was a drug addict who made some bad choices in life that ended up blessing me. My stepfather was a good hard-working man who loved alcohol, but he wasn't abusive. And my mama, God bless her, she was my rock, and she was always working her tail off.

So, I had to find that support within myself. Nobody was coming to see me play, but that made me stronger, and it told me a lot about myself. If I played a good game, I looked myself in the mirror and told myself I played a good game because no one else was gonna do that. As a result, I became SELF-RELIANT and STRONG-MINDED.

I knew who I was. But I had trouble figuring out OTHER PEOPLE in life. Who were THEY? I was running on a different type of fuel. I came to realize that not everybody thinks like me. Sometimes I felt like NOBODY thought like me. I was my own person, a different man who was moving different and thinking different than everybody else. And that was OK. I built up this dude inside me that had a burning desire to be GREAT with a tremendous work ethic and nobody was going to tell him he couldn't do those things.

It's hard to achieve your deepest desires when you don't know who you are. How do you get there? Sometimes, it starts with realizing who you are NOT. At this age and stage of my life, there's nothing that surprises me. I've identified my strengths and know when I'm at my best. I know where I'm going to dominate. But I'm also very familiar with my shortcomings. I know where I need help and I've ACCEPTED that.

So, where I'm SHORT, I'm gonna have a coach who is TALL. Where I'm BIG, I can have a coach who does other things but is short in the areas where I can give them assistance.

There's a profound saying in the Bible, "Thy rod and thy staff, they comfort me." I wouldn't be on this stage as the head coach at Colorado without a staff that comforts me. They CHALLENGE me. They COMPLETE me. They don't threaten me. I know who I AM and who I'm NOT, so my staff is going to help compensate for my weaknesses.

In Relationships, Just Be You

Every time these kids arrive on recruiting visits to Colorado—after every other school is trying to woo them and shower them with adulation—I just tell our whole staff, "Let's just be us." When you can authentically be who you are, that's winning and freeing. Feeling secure to JUST BE YOU in your relationships, that's true happiness.

Now, when the parents come in, I'm going to turn on the Prime switch. Of course I am. I've got to be Prime for them. They're usually forty, fifty, maybe sixty years old, and they probably were fans of mine when I was a player, so that's what they expect. Those parents have seen our *Coach Prime* documentary. They're looking for a little Prime and we give that to them. But we don't have to PARADE them around and put on a show.

There's a reason why we brought in their son. We've ALREADY identified him as somebody who's a fit, somebody who can help us succeed. They don't need a show. They need us to BE WHO WE SAY WE ARE—coaches who get sent a boy are expected to produce a man. Now, that boy may not always be happy with the way we do things, but he's going to be a man and a professional. Maybe not a professional football player. But he's gonna be sitting in the room of GAME CHANGERS and WINNERS who will bring solvency to our country's progress.

The fans will know these guys for what they do on the football field. But that's no way for them to know who these guys REALLY ARE. Can you imagine if the world had the opportunity to see you AT YOUR BEST for two or three hours a day? Your profile would be so enhanced. Everything would be so DIFFERENT and WONDERFUL because people would reach all their conclusions about you from those two or three hours.

That sums up the life of a college or professional athlete. But what happens during all the other times, the so-called trappings of life? That's when the PROBLEMS can occur.

We must SEPARATE the games from life's realities. We have to be the role models—not just models playing a role—and teach our guys that being their authentic selves is OK.

My mama was my role model. She was ALL THAT and a bag of chips in my eyes. It's cool to think your role model is an athlete you don't really know because there are some outstanding examples being set, but I ALWAYS think it's better when you have a role model you can actually touch and see how they conduct themselves day in and day out.

Be CAREFUL who you follow. Be CAREFUL who you look to as a role model. Look to the people you can reach out and touch, the people who are OK with you being your AUTHENTIC self. In relationships, JUST BE YOU.

Build Your Unique Brand

You know the problem most young people have with being true to themselves? It's tough to be authentic when you're trying to portray yourself as something different on social media.

I already hear what y'all are saying. "Hey Coach, you were called 'Prime Time.' How AUTHENTIC was that?"

Yeah, I got you. But here's the true story on that. I had a purpose to better myself. First and foremost, all these people now who are busy building their BRAND, their priority should be building their GAME or their REPUTATION.

You might be thinking . . . *Brand? What does that have to do with me?* Let me tell you: Everything! Whether y'all realize it or not, you have a brand, and it's all about how you present yourself to the world.

The first thing y'all need to do is figure out what your brand is. What do you WANT people to associate with you? Are you a hard worker? Are you creative? Are you PASSIONATE about a certain cause? Whatever it is, home in on THAT and make it your FOCUS.

Once that brand is identified, it's time to start building it. And the best way to do that is through your actions. It's not just enough to TALK the TALK. You gotta WALK the WALK.

If you say you're a hard worker, then put in the extra hours and show your boss what you're made of. If you're passionate about a cause, get involved and make a difference.

Your appearance and the way you communicate are both VERY KEY to your brand. Always present yourself in a way that ALIGNS with your brand.

For you creative folks, don't be afraid to express that through your clothes or accessories. I learned that early—it always pays to ACCESSORIZE!

And when you're communicating—these days, that might be more online than face-to-face—make sure you're representing your brand in a POSITIVE way.

You know what might be most important? NETWORKING! You gotta have CONNECTIONS, people, and you gotta WORK THEM. You also gotta go to events in your industry (some are actually FUN), join professional organizations, and be active on social media.

That's what I'm teaching my son Bucky when he goes with me to speaking engagements. He's there to record everything for social media, but I teach him how to work a room.

You start with the main people, then you hit the perimeters. Then you go in reverse. And by that time, everybody in the room has been touched. I tell Bucky we've got to use the personal touch. Call somebody by their name if you can. Find something to compliment them about. *Hey, those are some beautiful earrings. Man, where did you get that tie?* All that stuff is important. It gives you presence and it shows that you carry yourself the right way.

Your brand needs to be AUTHENTIC and a reflection of who you truly are—not who you think you should be. Don't try to emulate somebody else's brand just because you think it will make you successful. That's playing make-believe. Embrace your unique qualities and let them shine.

Do all that and you're on your way to showcasing your BEST SELF to the world!

Always Be a Good Teammate

The truth of the matter is I'd rather go to the office and seclude myself, just engulf myself in trying to be DOMINANT in what we do. If I had my choice, I'd rather not be in a crowd.

But I know I can't isolate myself. And you can't either. Look, I know y'all work hard every day for your cash, but it's not just about working hard. It's about working TOGETHER.

We've talked about finding yourself as an individual. But no matter WHO YOU REALLY ARE, you absolutely gotta learn to be part of a TEAM.

A team is only as strong as its weakest link. If you're not a good teammate, you're hurting the whole squad.

Let's break this thing down:

First, being a good teammate means being RELIABLE. If you say you're going to do something, DO IT! Don't leave your teammates hanging. And if something comes up and you CAN'T deliver, COMMUNICATE THAT ASAP. Don't let them find out at the last minute that they're gonna miss their deadline because you DROPPED THE BALL. Not cool, y'all. Not cool.

That leads to my next point:

Being a good teammate means being a good communicator. That means talking it up. Yes, it does. But it also means LISTENING. Don't interrupt your teammates. Don't DISMISS their ideas. Give them your darn RESPECT! If you got an issue, bring it up in a CONSTRUCTIVE way. Don't you dare complain or gossip behind their backs.

So y'all need to be positive toward your teammates. Nothing kills the mood faster than NEGATIVITY. I don't care if you think your work stinks. Maybe it does. That's just the way it is, folks. When you're at work, you leave that stuff at the door. Your energy is CONTAGIOUS, so make sure it's a good kind of energy.

So now that you're all in on the team, one more thing. And this is a BIG one. You gotta help when you're needed. Don't retreat to the office with your door closed. If you finish your project early, don't just SIT THERE and watch your teammates struggling. Offer to help. Or at least ask them what they need.

That's just plain RESPECT. You've got to respect your teammates' time, opinions, and personal space. Don't interrupt them when they're busy. Don't tear down their ideas. Don't get in their area without permission. All of that is just COMMON COURTESY, y'all.

This is stuff you learn as a kid. Should I even say the next one?

Yeah, I need to say it. CLEAN UP after yourself and don't be THAT PERSON who leaves trash everywhere.

One focused person can do GREAT things. But a focused TEAM? Oh my goodness! You take my word for it and write this down. If y'all do all this stuff the right way and take care of each other, they'll be calling you the DREAM TEAM around the office.

You know what to do. Go get it!

COACH PRIME'S TAKEAWAYS

1. **Don't go HIDING behind a costume or a false front.** Find out who you really are and be consistent with that. Embrace it. Don't be fake. Be authentic. Be YOU!

2. **Know who's on your team.** Do they share your values? Do they have your back? If you got the right folks, keep them CLOSE to you.

3. **Figure out your personal brand and PROMOTE it.** Make sure it reflects what's important to you. Do you want to be known for hard work? Creative flair? Passionately supporting a cause? Then COMMUNICATE that— relentlessly.

4. **Don't do this alone, y'all. Build a good NETWORK of people** and don't be scared to work your CONNECTIONS.

5. **If you're on a team, you gotta be a good TEAMMATE.** We're not looking for a LONE RANGER. We don't want TONTO either. You gotta be reliable, positive, a good listener, and a HELPER. Trust me. Do that stuff every day and those other folks will LOVE having you as a teammate.

CHAPTER 8

Make Sure Your Team
Is Better with You on It

*W*hat do YOU bring to the table?

The table we're talking about here really doesn't have anything to do with food, but it does sort of remind me of a dinner party or a family get-together.

When I come to a table like that, I'm bringing sandwiches or drinks. Somebody else might bring the ice or dessert. The goal is making sure there's enough of everything to go around. That's not the responsibility of just one person. A complete meal that's being served at that table is the work of an entire team of people.

Inevitably, there's always THAT ONE PERSON who shows up with one thing and one thing only.

Their appetite.

They literally bring NOTHING to the table. That's a TAKER. That's someone with no consideration for anyone but themselves. Ultimately, that's someone you can do without, someone who won't at all be missed during the next gathering.

That's NOT who you want to be. That's NOT the reputation you want attached to your name.

You want your team to be better when you're on it. Everybody should come to the table with something that creates value. We hear a lot about power couples. You will never be a power couple if just one of you has the power. Power couples exist because both have tremendous value that they bring to each other. They have valuable gifts, and when you combine them, it makes for something powerful and rare.

You weren't put on this earth to fill a seat or check a box. You should raise the temperature of the room by making yourself special and adding value to the cause. And if you're suddenly removed from the picture, people should look around and wonder what happened. Your presence should be missed.

The truth is . . . you MATTER. Sometimes, we don't understand the significance of how much we matter. It's almost like we don't fully appreciate someone until they're gone. If they brought us VALUE, if they gave their TALENTS, they will be MISSED greatly.

You should have that kind of impact on most everything in your life. It's not about your position or your job title. All that does is identify you. It doesn't tell anything about your value or the effort you put in.

It was Dr. Martin Luther King Jr. who said, "If a man is called to be a street sweeper, he should sweep streets as Michelangelo painted, or Beethoven composed music or Shakespeare wrote plays. He should sweep streets so well that all the hosts of heaven and earth will pause to say, 'Here lived a great street sweeper who did his job well.'"

Ordinarily, people wouldn't even notice a street sweeper, right? But according to Dr. King, this particular street sweeper made such an impression with their work—and I'm also guessing there were great interpersonal skills on display—that they made themselves unforgettable and indispensable.

That's a street sweeper with VALUE.

Remember when you were a kid on the playground or at recess? They would pick teams for the game. Well, somebody had to be picked last or second to last or third to last. And if that person was YOU, it kind of hurt.

You still got to play, but it probably stung if you were chosen last. As if you had no VALUE—or at least no PERCEIVED value.

Now when the game started, that was an opportunity. You had a chance to CREATE some value for yourself and show that you were an asset. And if you played well, you probably were a high pick the next time around. You were suddenly perceived as VALUABLE.

You were the same person. So what changed?

You made your team better.

Do (More Than) Your Job

We've all seen those sideline videos of Bill Belichick talking to his players recovering on the bench. He's usually a man of few words.

"Do your job."

It doesn't matter whether the player is struggling or dominating. Coach Belichick's message stays simple.

I understand what he's saying. Don't make things too complicated. Don't overextend yourself and worry about things outside your control. Just, you know, do your job.

But when it comes to being valuable, when it comes to making sure your team is better with you there, I think you need to ask even more of yourself.

Don't just do what's expected of you. Don't settle for average.

Be a GAME CHANGER!

I know many of you, when you were hired, had a job description that came with your position. It outlined your responsibilities and gave you a sense of the necessary qualifications. I think those sorts of boundaries often lead to a mentality that doesn't exactly allow you to grow.

"That's not my job, man."

"Well, what you're asking me to do is way above my pay grade."

You want to make yourself valuable? You want to be truly special? Do MORE than your job. Expand your horizons. Take on some new responsibilities. Under-promise and over-deliver.

I've seen plenty of people who are content to just do their job, but that's never a way to achieve at an elite level. I've also seen people who are willing to go the extra mile, and they are always the ones who turn out to be memorable.

Here's why it's important to do MORE than your job:

It shows that you're AMBITIOUS. You're not happy with just coasting along. You want to be the BEST and you're willing to put in the work to get there.

It shows that you're RELIABLE. People can count on you and you're not going to flake out on your responsibilities.

It shows that you're a TEAM PLAYER. If you were just thinking about yourself, you'd be clocking out at quitting time and not worrying about the stuff that hasn't gotten done. But when you're thinking about the big picture—when you want to make your team even better—you can't tolerate anything less than your standard.

It shows that you're HUNGRY. That you're not looking for the status quo. That you want to keep getting better.

Doing more than your job isn't for everybody. If it was, everybody already would be doing it. It's for the people who are serious about being GREAT.

And I love that!

Some of your coworkers might be miffed at your outward display of ambition, maybe because you're making them look bad. Ignore it. There's an old saying that goes, "You will never be criticized by someone who is doing MORE than you. You will only be criticized by someone who is doing LESS."

By going that extra mile and taking on more responsibility,

you're proving to be one of those people who puts the team first. That's how to make your team better.

Establishing Some Value

In a hypercompetitive world, especially when the skills and qualifications are close to equal, how can you make yourself stand out?

You've got to understand your gift.

Everyone has a gift. You work on your gift. You perfect your gift. Then you present your gift. And that's how you become known.

My gift of athleticism was already there in high school. When I got to the next level, I perfected it. Then it was packaged and presented to the whole country in this marketing ploy where I became known as "Prime Time."

When an agent gave me a pamphlet showing how much everyone made in the NFL—and how defensive back was among the worst-paid positions—I couldn't fathom that. My whole goal was to make enough money to retire my mama forever.

I knew I had to do something extraordinary to uplift defensive backs. My nickname allowed me to come up with something profound and prolific to package. By creating a character and a persona that was so far detached from who I really am, I brought a lot of attention to myself.

And that's how the goal was accomplished. People couldn't wait to watch. I stood up and stood out.

Those were the moments that set up the rest of my life. That is where I established my value. And that's what you need to do in order to achieve your success.

It can't be just a job. It can't be just a punching of the time clock.

To be the best, you must do the things others are unwilling to do. That's going to require thinking outside the box, coming up with new ideas, and being able to solve problems.

The world is constantly changing and so is the workplace. If you're open to new ideas, learning new skills, and taking on new challenges, you will make yourself into someone of great value.

Here are some other ways to increase your value:

- **Bringing out the best in your teammates**—It's valuable to know your teammates, their strengths and how to position them for success.

- **Sacrificing your ego**—When you set aside personal agendas for the good of the team, you create value by accepting your role and working to become the best possible version of yourself.

- **Showing respect**—Instead of doing your own thing, it's valuable to listen, be on time, and have a superior attitude while following the plan.

- **Leading by example**—You can exemplify the value of a winning culture through your own character, commitment, and work ethic, while showing a great example through your nonstop effort.

- **Being reliable**—There's nothing more valuable than people knowing you can be counted on, because they see you showing consistency and follow-through.

- **Competitiveness**—Who doesn't love internal fire, high standards, and pushing teammates toward continual improvement?

- **Being a positive force**—If you lift the spirits of your group, if you give them enthusiasm and encouragement, if you possess the kind of energy that creates positivity and confidence, your value will be obvious.

Be a Connector

When someone graduates from college, family and friends practically stand in line to offer advice about the best way to make it in the world. There's no surefire method, but here's one of the most practical bits of information I've ever heard—and it's not exactly a news flash.

It's not WHAT you know, it's WHO you know.

But to me, it's even more than that. It's using your personal network for the GOOD. You want to be a CONNECTOR, someone who brings people together for everyone's mutual benefit. That's good for business. It's also good for humanity.

Because truly, we're all in this together.

I love how John C. Maxwell, the bestselling author and one of the top voices I've ever heard on leadership, describes his relationships:

"In my organization, I don't have employees; I have teammates. Yes, I do pay people and offer them benefits. But people don't work for me. They work with me. We are working together to fulfill the vision. Without them, I cannot succeed. Without me, they cannot succeed. We're a team. We reach our goals together. We need each other. If we didn't, then one of us is in the wrong place."

When someone new is hired at your office, do you introduce them around? Do you take them to lunch and learn about their path? Do you make them feel welcome?

Do you have a friend who might be a great sales lead for one of your teammates? Have you introduced them yet?

If you're doing a school group project, are you identifying everyone's skills and talents, then finding the best way to put them to use?

Is there a business out there offering a product or service that could help put your company over the top? Have you connected the key people?

It's impressive to show you have a substantial network of contacts and friends. But it's even more impressive when you show how willing you are to SHARE those relationships in order to help others.

As a leader, it's not important for you to take credit. In fact, it's better if you DON'T take credit. In most cases, it's not about WHO'S right. It's about BEING RIGHT.

Every team, organization, classroom, or family I've ever known has leaders and stars who are easily identifiable. But the most successful groups always have that priceless commodity flying under the radar, that underrated person who makes it all work so smoothly. They get along with everyone. They have the right instincts and don't care who gets the credit. When it matters most, they know the right thing to do and the right thing to say.

These are the connectors. They put people together in a special way and forge the bonds that transform good organizations into great ones. Every single day they find ways to make their teams better.

If you're not one already, you can become a connector. Even if you're not someone who enjoys social interaction, it's important to push out of your comfort zone and grow.

You build relationships one person at a time. It starts by being friendly and making a connection. Give someone a smile and a kind word. Find something you have in common. Ask questions of people to find out more because people LOVE talking about themselves. Tell people a little about yourself and be sincere when you're describing what's important to you.

Where do you find these people? When you get involved in LIFE—whether it's through picnics, conferences, events, fundraisers, neighborhood gatherings, parties, or Little League games—there are so many opportunities to connect. Challenge yourself by trying to talk to three new people each day. Or at least, each week.

It won't be long before you'll have a great network of people you can call on. The bigger your network, the bigger your vision. It can be great for business, but it's even better for your life.

COACH PRIME'S TAKEAWAYS

1. **ALWAYS find ways to bring something to the table.** Be a giver, not a taker. Find ways to develop skills, talents, and connections that can benefit others.

2. **Dedicate yourself to being the BEST at what you do.** Take pride in what you are producing. Even if you are assigned mundane, seemingly inconsequential tasks, make them SING with quality.

3. **Do your job well. In fact, do MORE than your job.** Don't be satisfied with the status quo or being average. Make yourself invaluable by becoming a GAME-CHANGER.

4. **The world is constantly changing and so is the workplace. If you're open to new ideas, learning new skills, and taking on new challenges, you will make yourself into someone of great value.** You must do the things others are unwilling to do. That's going to require thinking outside the box, coming up with new ideas, and being able to solve problems.

5. **Become a connector of people.** When you build an impressive network of contacts and friends—then use those connections for the greater good—that's an ideal way to bring value to your team or organization.

CHAPTER 9

Iron Sharpens Iron

If you put my all-time best athletic moments together, you'd have a pretty darn good highlight reel.

We can start with the back-to-back Super Bowl championships. Got me a pick in the first one and caught a 47-yard pass in the other. Earned me a couple of rings.

In my NFL career, I took nine interceptions, six punt returns, and three kickoff returns to the house. I might've done a little dancing after some of them.

Let's not forget baseball. One season, I led the National League with fourteen triples in just ninety-seven games. I batted .533 in the 1992 World Series. Oh, and there was that time when I played an NFL game in Miami, hopped on a plane, and suited up for a baseball playoff game in Pittsburgh that night.

I HATE starting off all these sentences with the word "I." But I was HIM. I was PRIME TIME. I had a good run—and a lot of fun.

But the most competitive, fierce, proud, nerve-racking moments I felt won't ever be found on a highlight tape. Let's look a little deeper. Let's go to the places few people see. We're all familiar with the places of glory and celebration. But let's go to where the work actually gets done.

I've always considered myself a hard worker because that's what I saw in my mother. I take the preparation VERY seriously.

My approach has always been to treat practice like a game, so the game would be like a practice.

Let's go back to 1994. It's a typical Wednesday afternoon during, let's say, mid-November. We're at the San Francisco 49ers' facility in Santa Clara, California. There are no screaming fans, no television cameras, nothing at stake except getting in the game plan for Sunday.

But for me, it was just like a mini Super Bowl.

Every practice, I was covering my teammates, including Jerry Rice—the best wide receiver to ever do it—and John Taylor.

Now, me and Jerry faced each other like ten times over the years, when my Falcons and Cowboys played against the 49ers. I got him. He got me. They interviewed us about it one time and we both had the same answer. Neither of us slept very well the night before those games. We were SERIOUSLY jacked up.

That 1994 season was different, though. Me and Jerry were teammates, and we won a Super Bowl together. But the road to that championship was paved every day, brick by brick, and neither one of us took a day off.

You could've done a documentary about those practices. I would've opened it with a Bible verse:

Proverbs 27:17—*As iron sharpens iron, so one person sharpens another.*

Iron sharpens iron.

Jerry brought out the best in me. I think I brought out the best in Jerry.

Y'all need that kind of good pressure in your business. Y'all need that kind of accountability in your family. Ya'll need that kind of accountability—period.

Shoot for the Best

First, let me caution you.

We all want to win, right? We all want to elevate in order to dominate, right? You see this happen in football quite often. You have a good team that's playing a so-so schedule. They're running up the score. They're unbeaten. They think their team is unstoppable. Then come the playoffs—with the real competition—and they lose.

What the heck just happened?

The whole darn season was a FALSE comparison.

We're always measuring ourselves against someone else. It could be your sibling. It could be a coworker. It could be a teammate. But if you're going to measure yourself like that, if you're going to compare, MAKE SURE IT'S TO THE BEST. Don't be satisfied to compare yourself against someone you can overtake within a month if you just do A, B, and C. It has to be the best. I didn't just want to be great. I didn't just want to be good. I wanted to be the ABSOLUTE BEST.

At football practice, we coaches call it "good on good" when the number one offense goes up against the number one defense. That probably gives a true measure of how GOOD we are at all the positions. When our scout team is facing our number one defense, its whole mission is to give the best possible look to our guys. The defense needs a realistic look, a point of comparison that it can use for preparation. You can't compare our scout team to our number one offense, but it needs to be the best possible version of itself to provide some valuable competition.

Who do you compare yourself to? Did you grow up with a big brother who always whipped you in sports, never letting up, maybe teasing you to the point of tears? Are you working alongside someone who's up for the same promotion, so you can't afford to zone out at the office? Do you have a mentor who's showing you the best moral, ethical, and spiritual way to live your life? Those are the comparisons that will make you better.

I'll be honest, though. We need to be careful with the comparison game in this social media age. You're looking at your friend and all these beautiful photos. They're portraying this perfect life, all this money they're supposedly making, how their kids are making straight A's and getting into the best colleges, how nice their home looks. Some of that might not be the complete picture or even be true, but we let it get under our skin. We get mad and sulk and wonder, *What's wrong with me? Why can't I be that perfect? Why can't I be like them?*

That's the society we live in these days. We're all basing our success and our self-worth on someone else's—what they have, what we don't have. And we may be measuring ourselves against a really flawed character that we don't even know, maybe somebody we see on TV, a person we'll never meet.

The best competition you'll ever face in your life?

Look in the mirror.

It's you.

Living Up to Your Standard

When I got to the point of practicing where I really wanted to be, I found out I wasn't competing against Jerry Rice. It wasn't even Michael Irvin. It was not even Andre Rison, or any of the guys from my era, even though some of them will go down as the best receivers in the history of the game.

It was me—all me.

There's only one you—ever. You've got skills and talents like no one else. You get to the point where you know your standard of excellence, so you're measured against yourself. And when you reach that point, you see your life in very different terms.

If I was facing Jerry Rice or Michael Irvin and I held them without any catches for a few possessions, everybody would automatically quantify that as a big success for me. But my criteria for success was VERY different. When I went back and watched the film, I could see that the quarterback had me in a bad spot but chose not to throw the ball my way. Or such fear had been placed in his heart based on what he had seen me do to a multitude of other quarterbacks that he didn't even try me. Or maybe the receiver got a step on me, maybe he had a clear route to the end zone, but he dropped the football.

Everybody else would look at the stat sheet and make their conclusions on what kind of game I played. Me? I had my own criteria. I knew deep in my heart whether I was living up to my own standard. That's the NEXT LEVEL we all need to reach in order to be our best. You're competing against your best yesterday and trying to reach an even better tomorrow.

The reality is you can only do your best—whatever that is— and you probably know when you've reached that level. It's something I always demanded from my kids. I didn't want them to try and be me. They didn't have to be the best on their team. But I needed them to give me *their* best.

There's a select group of people who are realistically shooting to be the next Oprah or the next Michael Jordan. Those are rare people. Their best is somewhere up in the stratosphere. For most people, it's about giving their best in school, giving their best on the job, giving their best with the role they have on their teams.

You've probably heard the phrase "phoning it in." I hate that phrase. It means that somebody's going through the motions, not even trying, not even caring. That's a big problem. We all need goals, and we all need to be moving in a positive direction.

Get in the Game

When I was with the Cowboys, I remember playing in a game at the old Texas Stadium. When I looked into the stands, there were more than seventy thousand people. There were probably a few hundred people there to talk about the game or write about it. There were cheerleaders in close proximity, wearing their uniforms, dancing on the sidelines. There were a bunch of coaches giving instructions in their headsets, analyzing what was going on.

They all had opinions. They all had jobs to do. They were all part of the show, part of the scene. It's the same at every football event, all the people around the periphery of the field.

But those people weren't in the game.

That was for the twenty-two players who were on the field. And not all those guys were actually IN THE GAME. Just because you're there physically doesn't mean you're IN IT. You gotta be in it to be in it. By that I mean physically, mentally, in a complete rhythm, in a zone.

Are you at home but your mind is still at work?

Are you in a marriage but really not in love?

Are you holding a position at your workplace but there's no way you're prepared for what that position requires?

Just wearing a helmet and shoulder pads and being on the field doesn't make you a player. You've got to PROVE it to me. You've got to SHOW you belong.

In our first spring at Colorado, none of our players were assigned numbers, but they did have their names written on their helmets. That made it a little tough on the coaches because we were getting to know a lot of the guys for the first time. But here's the deal: They had to EARN those numbers—by the way they practiced, by the way they took care of their business, by the way they worked with their teammates. You didn't get your number by accident. You EARNED it through PERFORMANCE.

I'll say this: Our players had a lot of pride in what they were doing for the team after they earned those numbers. That helped bring us together as a team. I guarantee you it showed every player that he wasn't going to be granted any kind of status until he showed it was deserved.

The Value of a Mentor

You might think you can do it alone in your business. Maybe you have tremendous experience and a great education. No doubt, that counts for something.

But you need a mentor. So do I. So does everyone.

You might not think it's that important, or maybe it's just for someone starting out in their career. But having someone to push you, show you the right way to go about things, or maybe just to listen to your problems and give you legit feedback, that's such an invaluable tool for your life and your life's work. It can be the difference between success and failure.

When I was starting out as a young football player, I had plenty of raw talent but wasn't sure at times how to harness it. When you're fast and athletic, you can get by. But we all need mentors or a coach. In sports, we call it a coach. In life, you call it a mentor. They both serve the same purpose.

Coaches and mentors can help you see things from a different perspective, while offering advice and guidance when you're feeling lost or overwhelmed. They can also give you a swift kick in the pants when you're slacking off.

My spiritual mentors have added special aspects to my life, especially when I felt lost and needed clarity. I spoke to Bishop Omar Jahwar, my pastor in Dallas, almost every day for years and years. He was always there for me, whether it was the trials and tribulations of life, problems within my team, family issues, or just being a wise presence when I was faced with a big decision. I was devastated in 2021 when Bishop Omar died after complications from COVID, but I am so grateful that Pastor E. Dewey Smith, from the House of Hope in Atlanta, has become my primary spiritual counselor. In the same way that I've always been sharpened athletically through my coaches and trainers, Pastor Smith sharpens me spiritually. He continually inspires me to be a Nehemiah, someone who encounters the ruins and builds it up to an even greater stature.

That's right. I want this book to inspire YOU. But I gain my strength from the people who inspire ME.

Even if you have a great job, you're making a substantial income, and you think everything is going great, you can still use a mentor. That person can help you unlock your full potential and achieve things you never thought were possible.

Some of you might be thinking, *Well, I don't have a mentor and have no idea who that could be, so I guess I'm just out of luck.* Don't make this too complicated. Mentorship doesn't have to be some formal arrangement. It can be as simple as finding someone in your everyday life that you respect and admire and asking them for advice or guidance.

It could be a coach, a teacher, a coworker, a family member, or even a friend. Sometimes, it might be someone you admire from afar, like a celebrity or a successful business leader. Maybe you can't meet them in person, but you can read about them, watch their interviews, and learn from their example.

I was extremely lucky when I found a mentor in the person that I had come in to replace. When I was a rookie with the Atlanta Falcons, my teammate was Bobby Butler, a cornerback out of Florida State, just like me. Knowing I had come to Atlanta to take his job, rather than being defensive or dismissive of me, he sat me down and said, "This is the way things go in the NFL."

We're still friends to this day. He helped me. Bobby, aka Reverend Pressure, was a critical guy in our locker room. He turned his life around and gave his life to the Lord. When you see somebody living their life correctly, doing the right things, having a healthy relationship with his wife and kids—that just made a big impact on me. I learned by watching the consistency of his walk.

After that, I always felt an obligation to teach these younger men and try to reach them. Even when somebody WASN'T on my team—if they were a baller and they messed up—I'd call them and get them straight. I was always drawn to the younger players, the ones who sometimes got no attention, and I think that was because of the respect and help that Bobby gave me.

If you're lucky enough to find someone who's willing to mentor you, be grateful and show them that you're serious about learning from them. It takes some humility and realization that maybe you don't know everything and maybe you should be open to learning from others. Take their advice to heart, be respectful of their time and expertise, and don't take advantage of their generosity.

And then be sure to pay it forward and become a mentor to others in need. Together, we can build an unstoppable next generation.

COACH PRIME'S TAKEAWAYS

1. **You're always going to remember the significant moments in your life, the times when you succeed and feel like you're on top of the world. But you don't get to those places without some discipline or somebody pushing you** to find your potential. Nobody sees the preparation, but THAT is what sets you up for success.

2. **If you're going to measure yourself against someone else and compare, MAKE SURE THEY'RE THE BEST.** Don't be satisfied to compare yourself with someone that you can overtake within a month if you just do A, B, and C.

3. **The reality is you can only do your best—whatever that is—and you probably know when you've reached that level.** Sometimes you're NOT the best at something. But it's vitally important to always GIVE your best effort.

4. **It's easy to criticize from the sidelines. It's different when you're in the game.** So always have respect for the people in the arena who are making it HAPPEN.

5. **No matter where you are in your career and life, getting a mentor can be invaluable.** They can see things from a different angle and push you to be your best. If you're able to find the person who tells you what you NEED to hear, not what you WANT to hear, you've got one of the key elements that will allow you to win.

CHAPTER 10

Respecting Others

In one of our first meetings at Colorado, I had my special assistant, recruiting staffers, administrative assistants, social media specialists, trainers, and nutritionists all stand up in front of the seated players. These people also all happened to be women.

As our players looked at the faces of these very important behind-the-scenes members of our program, I wanted to be VERY clear and VERY pointed about their role and how they were to be treated.

"One thing I don't condone is disrespect. When you pass one of these ladies, I expect you to call them by their name or by their title. Find out which they prefer. But be courteous. Be gracious.

"Next up. If there's any dysfunction or obstruction with your girlfriend, your fiancée, or whoever, that's it. You're done here. Don't call me. Don't have your mama call me. Don't call the athletic director. It's a wrap. You understand that? We WILL respect women."

I was looking to set the right tone for our players. Almost EVERYTHING we do is filmed for our social media channels. So when we posted this little one-minute video message about how we treated women, we got a quick reaction:

Old school is good.
He's coaching up real men. Awesome.

Hope more coaches do things like this in the future.
Coach Prime, teach them! Some haven't been taught. Mold
  them into real men.
Coach laying down the law. Respect and discipline go a long
  way to a good life. Old school working here. Listen to him.
This is something that should be the first thing brought up
  in meetings at all schools.
Props to Coach Prime.

While I want the respect of women to be a cornerstone of our program, it goes deeper than that. We want to be known for respecting *people*. At every level.

What we're really talking about is love. It's hard for me to be disrespectful to a woman because of the way I love my mama. When I see any woman of a lower-paying position, it's all love. I think about how my mama had to work two jobs to make ends meet. When I see a woman struggling to get her sons to practice, I have amazing respect because I know she's making the effort and doing the best she can.

Women are oftentimes the shapers of young men's relationships. Men will always remember the things they witnessed in their childhood through the eyes of their mother. It often sets the tone for how they approach marriage. I've learned so much from women. Grandmothers are the matriarchs of the family. Mothers are usually the ones who hold everything together. That's truly what I believe.

When I exude love, it's because of my mama. She was the kind of mother who would always fix you a plate of food and make sure you had everything you needed. She never asked me for anything, never tried to manipulate me or force me to do something her way. Instead, she always prayed that I would have the kind of life I wanted.

I very much believe in equal rights for women. By presenting those women at the front of the room, I wanted the visual display to offer the idea, "OK, we understand you. We give you respect. We give you equal value. But we also want to put you on a pedestal. You deserve to be here. And we respect the role you play in this program."

I try to incorporate into everything we do those qualities that the women in our lives and program offer. We all understand respect. But like I said, respect is really love. The key ingredient in any relationship—whether it's player to coach, wife to husband, friend to friend, or family member to family member—is love.

We all want respect.

We all want love.

The Absence of Respect

If you don't have respect in your relationships—whether it's a marriage, a friendship, or even a trust between teammates—that can spell trouble.

How can lack of respect show up in these areas?

Sometimes, your ideas or opinions are devalued or shot down completely. Nobody likes being treated like that. You want to feel free and safe to speak honestly and speak your mind. When your ideas are ridiculed and dismissed, you tend to withdraw and the whole idea of "being a team" is ripped apart.

We all like to joke around, but sometimes it can go too far. If somebody talks about your appearance or something else you're self-conscious about, that's no way to have a respectful relationship. We should build each other up and have encouraging words.

Disrespect is like poison. It can settle in slowly, and before you know it, it takes over. If it goes on too long, it can affect your self-esteem and cause you to withdraw.

If you're feeling disrespected in your relationships, you need to address it head-on. Folks that hate confrontation are going to sweep things under the rug. That might seem convenient, but it doesn't solve the problem. It's always best to go at these things directly.

That's the way to communicate clearly and set the proper boundaries. It's possible the other person doesn't know how their actions make you feel, and they might adjust immediately. But if you consistently stand up for yourself, you'll take away one of the main weapons of a disrespectful person—making someone feel small.

Respect for Authority

Whether it's the military, an office, a household, or a football team, an organization usually has a chain of command. There are people in charge and people who must follow directions. Respect is a two-way street in these situations, and it's always necessary to keep things running smoothly.

Still, you're going to find those people who say, "I'm an adult! I don't have to listen to what they say or show respect to that person!" Those are usually the people who don't last too long in any organization.

It's a lesson most of us learn at an early age, although it really doesn't matter how old you are. Respecting authority figures is important. They are there to teach you, guide you, help you, and keep you safe.

Yes, authority figures are sometimes strict and harsh. They have the power to make you do things you really don't want to. But a huge part of being a well-rounded, responsible adult is following the rules and taking directions from others.

This applies to learning from your elders, too. Anybody with more age and experience can teach you a few things, even if you think they're old-fashioned and out of touch. You'd be surprised at the kind of wisdom and tips you can pick up from an older person.

If you don't agree with what an authority figure is asking, there are usually channels through which you can make your opinion known. What you DON'T want to do is undermine the leadership and instructions from somebody who is in charge.

When you respect authority, it teaches you discipline and responsibility, while helping to build relationships with others. Those are the qualities we need from everyone in an organization.

Respect for Servant Leadership

In the old days, nobody questioned the tactics of coaches. Players did what they were told and had very little freedom to change teams or show their individuality. The heads of businesses and corporations were all about the bottom line of their organizations—and the employees were often just cogs in the system that made it run. But now we live in an era of "servant leadership"—and I think that's a great thing.

By this very definition, whether it's Coach Prime or the CEO of a major company, leadership figures are there to serve others. We share power. We put the needs of our people first. We want our people to develop and meet their goals because that's when everyone performs to a higher level. When we reach our objectives, the credit is shared because everyone played a key role. That includes the leader, of course, but that person continues to troubleshoot and be open to others while always keeping the big picture in mind.

If you're a true servant leader—and I know most of my coaching colleagues have embraced this approach—you create a culture of mutual respect.

Respect for Yourself

We've talked about the importance of respect in a few areas. But here's one that doesn't get nearly enough attention: self-respect.

How you view YOURSELF impacts every area of your life—including relationships, family life, work, socialization, and the direction of your future.

The saying goes, "We're born alone. We die alone." Regardless of how big our circle becomes, we're still looking at the same person in the mirror each morning. How we feel about that reflection will likely set the tone for whether we succeed or fall short.

Most of us spend a lifetime learning how to value our skills, opinions, and sense of self.

How many times do we find ourselves questioning our own abilities and strengths?

Here's the question I have: If we LACK respect for ourselves, how can we DEMAND respect from others?

Now, don't get things all twisted.

Self-respect isn't some kind of ego trip, where you're puffing out your chest, promoting yourself, and thinking you're a genius. It simply means you're proud of who you are. And it means you don't expect to be perfect. You graciously accept your flaws or imperfections.

It also means you don't accept bad behavior from others. You have a standard for how you want to be treated.

We hear a lot about self-care these days—and that's a huge part of self-respect. You aren't a robot. You can't be going 100 percent every second of the day. There's no shame in taking care of yourself and allowing your brain to decompress.

Self-respect is also an indication of who you choose to be in your circle. If you are surrounded by positive, productive people who always have your best interest in mind, that shows a respect for how you're utilizing the limited time you have each day. If someone doesn't recognize your worth, then THEY are not worth your time. Cut that negativity from your life.

I've always felt that how I handle my mistakes is a great indicator of my self-respect. Truly, the only mistake you can make is NOT LEARNING FROM THEM.

We all make mistakes. Don't stomp on your self-worth and beat yourself up. Pick yourself up, stay positive, and move on with your life.

Self-respect is a gift we all give to ourselves. When we live with authenticity and integrity—instead of constantly trying to please others or present a fake reputation—that's when we discover true happiness and confidence.

COACH PRIME'S TAKEAWAYS

1. **When you boil it down, respect is love.** We all want RESPECT. We all want LOVE. So when you offer those qualities to other people, you are being the best version of yourself.

2. **If you don't have respect in your relationships, it's going to inevitably create problems.** Disrespect is like poison. It can settle in slowly, and before you know it, it takes over. If it goes on too long, it can affect your self-esteem and cause you to withdraw.

3. **Your opinion matters, but you must show respect to authority figures and not automatically reject their requests.** You have to learn RESPONSIBILITY and DISCIPLINE. Take that a step further and always respect your elders. The age and experience of an older person can provide an unbelievable amount of valuable knowledge—just by listening and learning.

4. **If you're running a company, a team, an office, or a household, learn from the lessons of servant leadership.** By SERVING others—and not solely dictating to them—you help them grow and become more productive. Your people will appreciate being shown that level of respect.

5. **Self-respect is an often overlooked—but extremely vital—part of respect.** How you view YOURSELF impacts every area of your life—including relationships, family life, work, socialization, and the direction of your future.

CHAPTER 11

Your Uniform Matters

People in uniform tend to be universally RESPECTED. And that's because A UNIFORM MAKES A STATEMENT. It brings an expectation of professionalism. It's something you can trust.

I respect our military service members. Same with the police. But I also respect the UPS man. I respect the FedEx lady. I respect the mail carrier. I respect the people who are consistently in uniform because, really, they are who keep this country running. They are doing it the way they've been instructed. They don't have time to play. They're meeting deadlines and they have an end goal in mind.

The uniform MATTERS.

The reason why I'm such a stickler for a uniform probably goes back to when I was a kid. My stepfather worked as a foreman for Wickes Lumber. And he put on a uniform every morning.

I suppose he didn't like it. He definitely didn't love it. And there were times that I'm sure he didn't want to clock in. Sometimes he was too exhausted. But nevertheless, I would peek out of my room and see him in his uniform, ready to go to work. I would always see him in the kitchen, getting something to eat before going to work. He was PROVIDING something for us. No matter how he felt, he fulfilled his duty to his family. That made an IMPRESSION on me.

We all respected policemen so much back in the day. In school, when they asked us to write down what we wanted to be when we grew up, of course I wrote a "professional athlete." But after that was a policeman, because you knew they meant business and they didn't stand for nonsense. That uniform meant something. When you're going through an airport and you see a person in a military uniform, you stop and look, almost reverently, because that uniform MEANS SOMETHING.

Now, not everyone has an assigned uniform. But what you choose to wear to your office, store, or place of business is often perceived as a reflection of WHO YOU ARE. You might be thinking, *Come on now, Coach Prime. How is a bunch of fabric really going to tell people about my attitude, my heart, and what I bring to my job? I'm not dressing up like a fake, just to make a good first impression.*

Listen to me now: A good first impression might be ALL YOU HAVE. People are sizing you up all the time. How you look might be the difference between somebody giving you their business or moving on to the next person. How you look and how you carry yourself is EVERYTHING.

It's like when you're looking for a house. Certain properties have what they call "curb appeal." Your real estate agent darn sure knows why that's important. You're attracted by the look. The grass is well kept. The shrubs are cut real nice. The house has a good coat of paint. It makes you want to stop and check it out. If it looked all unkempt, you'd keep on driving.

When it comes to how you present yourself, you don't have to be the best-looking person in the room. But you DO need to look YOUR best. That means making sure your clothes FIT properly. If you've gained some weight, don't be cramming yourself into something that doesn't fit. Y'all know what I mean.

You should always look put-together. Like you made an effort. Not rolled up in whatever you slept in or what wasn't in the laundry basket. That's true for your business. It's also true for our football team. Even at practice, our players aren't allowed to hit the field with just any type of socks. We don't tolerate any stuff hanging out. We don't allow earrings. There is an expectation that I have of them and that I expect them to have of themselves. Same goes for you.

The football uniform means something. You can hardly see what those kids look like because they're dressed up like warriors. But when you get a team running out of that tunnel, all looking the same, unified, the helmets shining, the jerseys tucked in, the socks pulled up, the shoes looking good, man, it's a good moment.

A football team is like a military unit. Both take care of their uniforms. Both RESPECT their uniforms. Both have a lot of pride in how they look. The colors and the logos show that we're all working together, trying to accomplish the same goal.

My coaching staff and I don't allow slides or slippers or pants sagging down or earrings or even hoodies. But sometimes you'll still hear some fool say, "I should be able to wear what I want because I'm an individual." Nope. You're not gonna see that one pant leg up, one pant leg down, looking like Flo-Jo, on my field. That's just stupidity.

Even in the classroom, in the cafeteria, or around campus, my players must look a certain way. No sleeveless shirts. I don't want to see your armpits. The entire Colorado campus is your home, not just the field house and stadium, and you've got to be prepared to make a good impression on anyone who might visit. I might have a CEO sitting in my meeting room one day. How will it seem if you show up looking all sloppy?

Everything we do has got to exude professionalism. While they all want to go to the NFL, the fact is, about 95 percent of my locker room will NOT go pro. We've got to get them ready for the real world. And how you look MATTERS.

Looking Good, Feeling Good

As you probably know, I'm rarely at a loss for words. I've pretty much got a quote for everything. But this one has always been one of my best:

"WHEN YOU LOOK GOOD, YOU FEEL GOOD. WHEN YOU FEEL GOOD, YOU PLAY GOOD. AND WHEN YOU PLAY GOOD, THEY PAY GOOD."

I still live by that today.

Hours before a game, I'll lay my entire outfit out—shirt, pants, shoes, socks, jacket or sweatshirt, even the baseball cap (or maybe the cowboy hat). I want to make sure it's all on point. When I'm satisfied that I've got all I need, then I'll start to get dressed.

Do y'all put that much thought and care into how you look? Or are you scrambling to grab whatever you see first?

Looking a certain way, that's my tradition. It started back in elementary school. I'd lay out my clothes the night before the first day of school. I'd take my time getting ready, and everything had to look just right.

When it looked right, I felt right.

I remember playing youth football, getting dressed at the crib, laying everything out so I could see how it would look, but also to make sure I wasn't forgetting anything, especially the accessories.

That continued right through to the NFL. There's a lot of downtime between when you arrive and when the game actually starts. You can go at your own pace. I know, especially in the beginning, you're so proud of your uniform. *You made it, man!* When I laid it out, took my time, and visualized what was about to unfold on that field, I usually balled out.

How many of y'all get that sensation when you go to work? You're wearing your favorite suit or outfit, the one that looks great and feels just right. It gives you that confidence. You make the sale, you hit all your quotas, do great in your presentation, you're feeling ON TOP OF THE WORLD.

Feels good, doesn't it?

I am absolutely convinced there's a connection between the way you look and the way you feel. My look-good, feel-good quote isn't just a bunch of words. I truly believe it.

I actually heard Odell Beckham Jr., the NFL wide receiver, speak on it:

"I believe it's a placebo effect or whatever you want to call it . . . there's a role in how you dress and how you perform . . . when you feel good, look good, you play good."

He also said he would get pictures of what he was going to wear the next week and try to get in the mindset of how it would look on the field.

I swear I didn't tell OBJ what to say. But I ABSOLUTELY agree with the man. Those words could've come right out of my mouth.

When I got to Jackson State, I made how we looked a big priority. We had a different uniform combination every week, and the players' names were on the back of the jerseys, a very big deal in the SWAC.

But the biggest thing we did was change the way we looked OFF the field. We teamed up with one of my business partners, Michael Strahan, the Pro Football Hall of Famer (you folks might know him better from *Good Morning America* or *The $100,000 Pyramid*), who has his own clothing line at Men's Wearhouse. We got custom suits for our entire football program.

Man, I was jealous of these kids. I didn't have my first custom suit until I was an NFL player, so these guys didn't know how good they had it! These were nice threads—navy-blue suits with Jackson State's logo in the lining and each player's name sewn inside the jacket. They also each got a set of ties from Chris Ellis of Prime Neckwear. Looks are important, and I wanted our players to take great pride in looking good, regardless of their family's income. I wanted to show them that you don't have to be rich or wealthy to look good. It starts with a state of mind. But a suit sure can help.

The minute they put those suits and ties on, I could instantly see how their attitudes changed. Deep down, kids don't want to look sloppy. They want to look GOOD. I was hearing they felt like they were grown-ups. They looked like important businessmen. They projected pride in their school and their program. They COULD NOT WAIT to put on those clothes and have people see them get off the bus.

Their uniform, in this case a suit, was a transformation of positivity, dignity, self-esteem, and self-respect. Beyond a game, these guys were ready for a job interview or maybe speaking to a company about an endorsement deal for themselves.

So, if we can CONTROL how we look, that's going to have an INFLUENCE on how we feel. And if we feel good . . . well, y'all know the rest.

So that famous quote I mentioned a few pages back — "When you look good, you feel good . . ." — y'all probably thought that was all about sports, didn't you? Because when I said it, I was in full Prime Time mode, wearing my shades and my mink coat. I apologize . . . my FAUX mink coat. You got to be careful nowadays.

Anyway, that quote is actually about YOU and your life. NEVER underestimate how your look can get you in the door with people. Never sacrifice that. Your style starts with you. We're not only talking about style. We're really talking about discipline.

A Life of Discipline

When we ran our TRUTH youth organization in Dallas, those kids were honored to be wearing the uniforms they were wearing. It made them feel like they belonged to something.

It was a MACHINE. And we built that darn machine. The five- and six-year-olds, they wore white bottoms and white tops with TRUTH on the leg, TRUTH on the chest. The seven- and eight-year-olds wore black bottoms and red tops. The nines and tens, they wore black on black. The elevens and twelves wore red on red. It was all organized and color-coordinated so that when we saw a kid running around, we knew where he was supposed to be.

We offered cheerleading and dance, too. We were teaching these kids life skills and giving them spiritual guidance. And it wasn't just the kids. It was the parents. We'd talk to the parents about how they SMELLED. If they reeked of alcohol or weed, that likely meant those parents were smoking or drinking the whole way over here. They had to set a better example for their kids.

And if they were late? We didn't blame the kid. That was YOU, Dad! The oldest kids in the program were twelve. They weren't driving. You better get them there on time out of respect for the coaches AND the players.

We'd make the dad get out of the car and run with the kid because he made the kid late. We'd tell our kids to make sure they got in the car in plenty of time, dressed in their uniform, even if they had to wait for their parents. Because if you're late, you don't get to play. Those kids didn't want to be late. They COULDN'T WAIT to get up and wear that uniform. They CRAVED that form of discipline. Eventually, all the parents straightened up.

Even those young kids knew what it was like to look good and feel good.

We helped show them the way. They developed the discipline. And it all started from the way they looked. They were part of something bigger, which made them feel special and gave them a sense of belonging.

I remember being so excited when I got to Florida State. My name was on the back of my jersey! We never had that in high school. We didn't have different uniform combinations. Now I got to represent my family. And my name was on my back. It mattered. It was a big, big deal. Another big deal was having the single-digit number. That was something you had to EARN.

Nowadays, all these kids think they're entitled to a single-digit number. Even the linemen want it. I tell my players that the number zero isn't available. Why does anybody want zero? That means you're nothing. And how you gonna be number one if you're not THE ONE? So, I decide who gets number one and I give that out. Number two isn't available. So, there are just seven other single-digit numbers and those are all special. We take how you look very seriously, right down to the number you're wearing.

At the college level, we're preparing these players for the next level. For a few of them, that's the NFL, where it's all about the discipline and structure, where all these things are mandated. For most of them, that next level is about stepping into real life. Wherever they land, they're going to need discipline to succeed. That starts with how you present yourself.

If they think they're going to matriculate into the job market and go to UPS and wear any uniform they please, no, that is NOT going to happen. And they won't get a warning. If they go to Wall Street and think they can just fall into the office and walk in there looking any way they want, they are sadly mistaken.

Within a team, within an organization, you've got to have that kind of consistency. And we've got to set the example.

Growing up, I had tons of respect for my favorite athletes. I was drawn to their professionalism and commitment.

I loved Dr. J—Julius Erving, the basketball player from the Philadelphia 76ers—because he was a consistently classy individual. The guy was one of the most acrobatic dunkers of all time, but he was a true leader and a great team spokesman who set a tremendous example.

I had great respect for Hank Aaron and remember the moment he broke Babe Ruth's all-time home run record. Hank Aaron had a quiet dignity about him. When did you ever see Hank Aaron out of pocket? He dealt with all that racism, but he was always locked in and never lost his focus.

Muhammad Ali, the greatest boxer of all time, was brash and cocky. He also had the comments to make headlines—and sometimes his lines even rhymed—but man, could he back it up!

Last but not least, O.J. Simpson. Not the O.J. YOU know, but the other O.J. that I GREW UP ON. In my era, Orenthal James Simpson was called "The Juice." And that's what he had. He had power, influence, success, likability from all ethnicities. He had endorsements and you'd see him in TV commercials and movies. Most of all, his linemen believed in him. They went the extra mile for O.J.

These were guys who looked the part. They dressed well. They were well groomed and articulate. If you took them off the ball field, the court, or out of the boxing ring, they could fit right into any office or boardroom.

You would never picture Julius Erving, Hank Aaron, Muhammad Ali, or O.J. Simpson in a situation where they weren't dressed for success. They could fit into any situation and COMMAND the utmost respect from everyone.

Those guys knew how to present themselves well. They had a PRESENCE. The world needs more people with true presence.

All of us fall into a rut sometimes, walking the familiar or easier path. We want to cut a few corners. Maybe we just want to feel comfortable and not worry about looking our best. Maybe our grooming isn't on point. We're just not having a good day and don't think our appearance is that important. Because who's going to notice?

Don't fall into that trap. You've got to know and appreciate what excellence looks like. You've got to set the expectations so that EVERYONE knows that excellence can be achieved, regardless of your situation.

I'll say it again.

When you look good, you feel good. When you feel good, you play good. And when you play good, they pay good. It always works.

COACH PRIME'S TAKEAWAYS

1. **Looking the best you CAN—and paying attention to your grooming—will always help your situation.** When we see someone well dressed, when we witness someone carrying themselves in a classy manner, we automatically feel like that person is IMPORTANT and deserving of our RESPECT. The reverse of that is when someone looks sloppy, like they don't care how they look, we may not pay attention to what they have to say.

2. **Looking good is an investment in YOU.** It's going to pay off to educate yourself in acquiring the right kind of clothes, regardless of your income. You can still look good on a budget. I guarantee you that those clothes will change the way you feel about yourself and give you some added confidence.

3. **If you're someone who wears a formal uniform, take PRIDE in that.** Whether you're a policeman, a fireman, the UPS man, the mailman, or someone in the military, you're an important part of our country. You make a statement every day and you deserve respect.

4. **People crave DISCIPLINE and being part of something bigger than themselves.** That can start from the way you look each day.

5. **Now that you look good and feel good, it's time to ACT good.** Introduce yourself. Work the room. Learn how to present yourself well. You not only look the part but act the part, too. I know you can do it!

CHAPTER 12

Your Time Is Your Most Valuable Coin

Every day we each get 24 hours to do our thing. That's 1,440 minutes—or 86,400 seconds.

Where we differ is in how we USE that time.

Are you efficient? Do you make the most of your time? Or do you waste it? Do you let distractions derail you?

The use of time is the ultimate separator.

When I played in the NFL, there was NOBODY faster than me. There were plenty who were bigger. Definitely some who were stronger. Maybe a few who believed they were smarter.

But there was one area where everyone in the NFL was equal—and it's the same equalizing factor at every workplace in the WORLD.

We all have the same amount of time.

They always say hard work and attitude are the things we all can control. But to me, time belongs on that list, too.

Time is money. I BELIEVE that, yes sir. We're usually obsessed with what's in our bank account or in our wallet.

But to me, your time is your most valuable coin. It's PRICELESS.

I have always been time-conscious. I had no choice. I played TWO professional sports—football and baseball—and their schedules overlapped at times. My time had to always be carefully allocated, down to the minute. At one point in my life, I only had two weeks off the entire year, and that was the period between the NFL Pro Bowl and spring training. I'd go straight from covering the world's best wide receivers to getting my hands ready to swing a bat. I could barely catch my breath.

I'm sure y'all are busy, too. With today's kind of workload and pace, I can't understand how ANYONE expects to be successful without a well-defined schedule or a plan.

My whole life, things have revolved around a tight schedule, and I PROTECT that time. My journey has NOT followed a straight line. I've gone from athlete to media personality to businessman to youth coach to motivational speaker to college coach — and now all those experiences are wrapped up in being a guy who can INFLUENCE the world and CHANGE LIVES. That is my WHY. That is where MY TIME is always best spent. That is the priority I protect the MOST.

If you're a new parent and you're just starting your career journey, I don't even have to tell you about time. There just isn't enough of it! Am I right? How can you take care of your family's needs AND work AND stay in good physical shape AND get your proper rest AND have some downtime to clear your mind?

Man, I can RELATE to that struggle. Part of it is knowing when to say NO. You must be firm with that, now. Don't stretch yourself like Plastic Man, 'cause eventually you are going to BREAK.

But the biggest thing is being SMART with your time and having a PLAN. Here's the overall deal, plain and simple, and it's true for all of us: You want to WIN in life? You've got to MANAGE your time.

Time ALWAYS seems short if you're a parent. YOUR dream is helping your kids achieve THEIR dream. It all goes by real fast. Time ALWAYS seems short if you're the boss. You can't do EVERY-ONE'S job for them, but you've got to teach them to be efficient. You've got to lead by INSPIRING them to greatness. But when you're getting your kids up and running, or you're training a new employee who doesn't get it just yet, or you're trying to impart your words of wisdom to the folks who need it the most, all that takes SO MUCH TIME. Make sure it doesn't drain you.

Most people don't know how to manage their time. That's why their plates always seem so full. I can't tell you exactly what to prioritize, because everybody's life and priorities are different. But you better pick out the most important things to you and MAKE THEM into those priorities or else you're just going to be spinning your wheels.

My time is valuable. YOUR time is valuable. We only get one shot at each day, and we got to be ready at go time for this thing called life.

You Must Have a Plan

Can you build a home without a plan? Of course not. So, if you're going to build a successful day, you better have some kind of plan.

My plan may not always be written out, but it's thought out, premeditated, precalculated. I just don't HAPPEN to do things. I've never built something that is profound without a plan.

Now, how does that look on paper?

Let's say I'm getting seven hours of sleep. That's a great night of sleep for me. I will be READY for my day with LOTS of energy. So, take away those seven hours. We're down to seventeen.

Now we're dealing with seventeen hours, and we've got to maximize that time. You need to eat, work out, shower, groom, get dressed, all that stuff. Let's give that three hours. Now we're down to fourteen hours to get everything else done.

I think that's a lot. I think that's PLENTY. So why do people get to the end of their day and wonder why they got NOTHING done?

Because they don't have a plan.

Because they don't value their time.

Because they WASTE that time.

If you want to maximize your time, everything you do has to be PURPOSEFUL. What's the priority of what you're doing right now? What's the purpose? How much time are you allowing for this task? If you can't answer those questions, THERE is your problem.

Don't spend your money on FOOLISH things. Everybody understands that, right?

Doesn't mean everyone does it, but most folks at least understand the idea. I'm telling you not to spend your TIME on foolish things. Wasting your time is like buying some meaningless trinkets down at the corner store. At least you get a receipt for the trinkets and you can take them back. Waste your time and it's gone forever.

My Time must be Prime.

Let me say that again.

My TIME must be PRIME.

And YOURS should be, too. Don't let people chime in with what you should do with your life and let them play around with your PRIME TIME. Protect it. Use it. DO NOT WASTE IT!

Set Goals and Compartmentalize

We all need to set goals—a way to prioritize and maximize our time. And it's cool to have a bunch of them on your list, so you can check the boxes and know you're getting stuff done.

But I've got an ULTIMATE goal—and that's what my life revolves around every single day.

My goal is to change the lives of young men.

When I look back at my journey—whether it was my playing career, finding my faith, being on the set at NFL Network, working with the kids in youth ball or high school, then getting my opportunity to coach in college—it's like I've banked all these valuable experiences and now I can withdraw them from the ATM.

It's not just the journey. It's the shift in my mindset. Sometimes you get enjoyment from an activity. But when you discover PURPOSE and TRUE SATISFACTION, that's when everything changes. When you learn why you were put here on this earth, and you start to realize the things you can ESTABLISH and leave behind for OTHERS, then you aren't just passing time. Every minute becomes an INVESTMENT in something that's very real.

My time isn't about ME anymore. Now it's about how I can use my time for others.

I'm a coach on the field and a dad at home. I'm a mentor to many. But in the eyes of most folks, I'm PRIME, and I need to deliver on that and show up even with all I've got going on outside the coaching world.

That's a lot.

So, you know one way I use my time to its maximum? I COMPARTMENTALIZE everything in my life.

It's funny how I've always done that. When I was younger, I'd have school, practice, games, homework. Everything had its own place and its own section in the day.

I even compartmentalize my food! You know how most folks mix the black-eyed peas with the rice? I NEVER do that. Can't stand it! Remember that lunchroom tray we all used to get back in the cafeteria? I used to LOVE those trays. Everything had its own compartment. The meat went here, the potatoes went there, the cornbread over here, and the little applesauce over there. That's how my life has always been. I always wanted to do things in order. I don't dabble in THIS until I finish THAT. I'm just built that way. And I normally don't drink anything until I'm finished eating. This probably seems WEIRD to some of you, but that's just one of the ways I organize my day. It makes things more efficient for me. I don't think I've ever wasted food. I know I've never wasted TIME.

In my world, everything has a time and a place.

If you've ever played for me, you figure that out IN A HURRY. I'm old school when it comes to the way we prepare. And if anybody deviates from that, if that causes us to take away from the time we should be using for preparation, then they've got a problem with ME.

I just don't play like that. I'm disciplined to a fault and very structured. We only have so much time to accomplish our goals. So, if I see somebody wasting that precious time, let me tell you, that's a GOOD way to get on my BAD side. Everything has its time and place when you are an organized and compartmentalized goal-setter.

Avoid Distractions

The Bible says that God uses the foolish things to confound the wise. We're all SURROUNDED by foolish things, but we've got to stay wise. We've got to be where we need to be so that we can get prepared for where we need to go. These days, that's a job in itself. I think some college kids are actually majoring in time-wasting.

Social media, as we all know, can be a great way to promote yourself. It can also mess you up. That click of a button can take down all the discipline you need for your day.

Are you on social media trying to edify others, trying to build something meaningful, trying to uplift? Or are you just fishing? Scrolling? Just meandering aimlessly and passing time with no point? Man, that social media will kill you. You are LOSING FOCUS. And when you lose focus, you lose TIME. And if you've been listening closely, you KNOW that is NOT the way to win at life.

Before practices and team meetings, after everyone gathers in the room, we usually give everyone five minutes on their phone, after which the phones are required to go up on the table and are claimed afterwards.

Before one of our games, we had a couple of fools on their phones. These guys were definitely not studying football. They were having a lengthy conversation about something totally unrelated on their social media feed. And I just WENT OFF. Those guys weren't with us for very long, by the way.

Look, man, I'm no different. I can be distracted. But I refuse to let that meaningless stuff creep into my life's routines. Instead, I work to keep myself insulated. When I start my day with an intentional plan, NOTHING is going to derail that. If you constantly react to the noise of life, you're never going to get anything done.

First of all, you got to identify what's noise to you. Because the same thing YOU call noise could be pleasant to ME. When I get to my office in the morning, I like a little Smokey Robinson and a little gospel. That's soothing to me. That's a good kind of noise for me because it sets the stage for my work. Some people can't focus unless there's complete silence. Other people seem to thrive on chaos, and nothing will distract them. Me? I need the focus, but the right kind of music puts me in a great mood and gives me energy.

Next, you've got to UNDERSTAND the mission and the goal. Then you've got to CLARIFY how you're going to get there. I'm a planner and I devise a plan. I don't just go to work. I PLAN my work. And then I WORK my plan. I do those things like no other—and I will not tolerate distractions.

Sometimes, you really must BLOCK everything out. I mean, you're ALONE at work, but your husband's there in your mind and he just got on your nerves. Or your wife's there in your mind and she's complaining about something that's supposed to happen next week. Or your kids are there in your mind and they came home late last night, so you're still mad.

You've got to FOCUS on that task and take care of the other stuff when it's time.

I don't have any tolerance for complacency or a super-slow pace. I like to do it RIGHT NOW. I deal with a God who's a right-now God. And so, I'm a RIGHT-NOW person.

Those people who like to sit around and procrastinate and go off topic or bring up subjects that have NOTHING to do with the task at hand . . . I don't work well with those folks.

You set your own pace. Once you get your people in place — whether it's your family or your coworkers — you identify what you want and how everyone's going to make it happen. You do this by COMMUNICATING your plan. Don't make anybody guess. Your folks aren't mind readers. You can talk it out. Or you can write it down — I like a nice orderly outline — so you "hand the plan" and avoid any confusion. If you have a family and an array of activities for the kids, it's essential to have a calendar where everyone can refer to what's ahead.

Once you've got the plan and everybody is on board, then you go. You just go.

You want ground rules? Don't accept EXCUSES. Don't allow PROCRASTINATION. Don't place BLAME. And most of all, DON'T DRAG YOUR FEET or WASTE TIME.

Just go get it.

The funny thing is, if you do everything you're supposed to do in the order you're supposed to do it, you ALWAYS have enough time. It's the people who aren't organized who always seem to be dealing with chaos.

Here's a tip: Find the time of day when you are most productive. Some of us are morning people. I know others who can't function too well until after lunch and then they're good! Don't waste time on the easy tasks that aren't that meaningful. If you have a few must-do tasks, the nonnegotiables, DO THEM FIRST.

Ever wonder why people always say if you want to get something done, give it to the BUSY person? That's 'cause those folks know how to USE their time instead of letting the time use THEM.

Being Productive

When it comes to time management, I'm all about making my time COUNT for something valuable. So, once you get that time management thing going good, your work ethic needs to keep pace.

When you're the head of your family, when you're a leader in your company, that comes with an OBLIGATION. It's up to you to be that cut man or woman in the corner. It's up to you to be that navigational system. When you're telling your people to make better use of their time, that STARTS with YOU.

We're all here on this planet in this life for a very short time, and we need to leave this world a better place than we found it. Use your time well. Got nothing to do? Then VOLUNTEER for something.

What separates you from others are the gifts you were blessed with and the decisions you make. A good decision can save you time. A bad decision can cost you time. Your decisions affect not only you but those around you. So, when you are making decisions on where to put your time and resources, that comes with a cost. You need to carefully weigh that cost—and make your time count for something valuable.

What I see for my own time is bringing people together, creating unity and provoking change. And I've got SO MANY ideas that there are plenty of times I wish there were thirty or more hours in a day.

I'm in my fifties, and a lot of people project about what I should do with my life. But I'm called to live MY dream. I felt the call to help kids, and before I knew it, when we started the TRUTH youth sports program back in Dallas, I was ALL IN. But you know what? I should've always known that was my destiny.

I saw my mama do this my whole life. This isn't something new. My mama has adopted and raised seven foster kids. That's who we've always been as a family. She was the best example simply by the way she led her life and conducted her business. My mama always made sure everybody ate, everybody had clothes on their back, everybody was doing right. Because of her I've always been that dude who makes sure my people are covered and provided for.

When there's a crisis or a need in my community, I don't run from it. I GET INVOLVED. So that's what I'm calling on y'all to do, too. We were put here for more than amassing a pile of money. If you got power, influence, position, connections, or resources, then you gotta USE THOSE THINGS for the greater good. While all the while maintaining that attitude of productivity.

When my kids wake up at 7 a.m., they're going to see their daddy is sweating from his workout. He's already eating breakfast. He's probably got a Zoom call scheduled soon. And the sun just came up. Yeah, that's what I like them to see. That's what I'd like EVERYONE to see.

Kids are usually very active and very competitive. But they take their cues from what they see, so you've got to be careful with the example you set.

My time is so valuable that I guard it like a bank vault. There's so darn much I want to do. You too? Hey, don't forget to carve out part of it to get your sleep and stay refreshed. They're not planning to add hours to the day. So how do you make it work?

I'll say it again.

YOUR Time must be Prime.

Take Nothing for Granted

Here's the reason why your time is your most valuable coin: You can't seduce it.

You can't manipulate it. Life can change in the blink of an eye. You aren't owed anything. Look, yesterday is gone. Tomorrow isn't promised. So every minute is like a precious gift. Your reward is getting the privilege of living the day you're in . . . and that's why they call it the "present."

You don't know how much time you have left, so be very careful when it comes to WHO you spend that time with.

Life is about moments. Don't take ANY of them for granted.

Are you going to be ready for your moments? Because when God shines that light on you, and life asks for a hand-up in that relay, you better run. You never know when that moment is coming. So you better be ready.

I didn't know I was gonna be thrown into the World Series against pitchers like David Cone. But I was READY for that moment. And when the lights were shining, I hit .533 in that World Series.

Moments are when you can separate yourself from the pack. Don't shrink when your moments finally happen.

Back in my hometown of Fort Myers, nobody was really dominating. I wanted to be different. I was willing to sacrifice and work my butt off. I knew that it would lead to the big moments I had to take advantage of.

A little while ago, I had a shoot for a Gillette commercial at my house, and my son Shilo was going to be in it with me. I said he could ride with me. He said, "No, I'm going somewhere first." I knew he was going to the club with his brother. So I said, "OK, but you know you got business. Don't be late."

He showed up to the shoot, but he was ten minutes late. I told my people, "You dock him for that time." He has to learn good stewardship. This was real business. This was SERIOUS.

So I'm prepping for the shoot, reading my stuff and thinking about how best to approach what I'm being asked to do. I'm being Prime. Shilo had seen that his whole life, but he had never seen me doing what I do, just turning it on instantly for the cameras, nailing the script perfectly, putting my personality into it and making it memorable. He had the same opportunity, but instead, he's just fumbling and stumbling over his lines. Totally unprepared. It was an embarrassment to himself and to me. And it was DISRESPECTFUL to everyone at that shoot.

I got on him and made it clear that you DON'T waste your opportunities—or other people's time. When you're sitting back there as the backup dancer, having your fun, you BETTER be ready when God calls you up front to get your solo. Shilo got the message. He studied his butt off and got it right the next day. But we still docked him for being late. I think he learned a valuable lesson about taking care of your BUSINESS.

So, I'm gonna REPEAT this for all y'all.

Don't waste your time.

And when it's time for your moment—BE READY!

COACH PRIME'S TAKEAWAYS

1. **TIME IS MONEY.** When you waste your time, you waste your money. That's why time is your most valuable coin.

2. **Get yourself a plan for each day.** Change the plan if necessary—hey, life will throw you a curveball now and then—but put some purpose into your day. THAT'S how you get things done.

3. **Everything has its own TIME and PLACE.** There's a time for work. There's a time for play. Don't get those mixed up.

4. **Plan your work. Work your plan. Working hard without direction usually gets you NOWHERE.** Don't let distractions or procrastination get in the way. Social media? Use it to edify and educate, not as a time-waster or day-killer.

5. **Start early. It's amazing how powerful you can feel when you get a lot of stuff done before the sun comes up.** Be productive. Volunteer. It will make you feel great about yourself. Your time is PRICELESS.

CHAPTER 13

What's Your Rabbit?

Back home in Fort Myers, I was fascinated with the dog track. Yeah, they used to have them all around Florida. You'd bet on the race, like the Kentucky Derby. Except instead of horses these were greyhounds. Even though I was too young to go because of the gambling, I had a sneak peek a few times. Beautiful dogs—all lean, athletic-looking, determined. Man, they looked like track stars.

They'd put those greyhounds into the chutes. And they'd put a mechanical rabbit just inside the curb and the dogs would chase the rabbit as the rabbit set the pace. It's an all-out quick race.

So here are the questions I have for y'all:

What's your rabbit?

What are you chasing? Are you going all-out after anything?

Or are you just running in circles?

I'm not talking about just catching the rabbit, although that would be nice. I'm talking more about being prepared for the opportunity to GO GET that rabbit.

Sometimes, you only get one opportunity to make something yours. You just have to take it. The only reason some of us are where we are today is because we made the plays.

Magic Johnson, when he had the chance, he made the plays. Now, he missed a few shots in his career, too. But when it really mattered, it seemed like that dude always made the plays.

In business, when you have a deal to close, you best close it. Surgeons, you've got to handle your business. Your hands must be steady. There's no making a mistake.

Everybody's chasing something. Most people are chasing success or financial security. They might be chasing a date or a future spouse. What's most interesting is what we do with that thing we're chasing once we get it. Because sometimes you mess around, you get your prize, then you realize you've got to go get another one. That first rabbit might not satisfy you like you thought it would.

So, it's never just about that rabbit.

The bigger question: What's your WHY?

When I was seven, I told my mama I was going to be rich and make a lot of money when I got older and that she was never going to have to work another day in her life. She looked at me, shook her head, and said, "OK, until then, go get the lawn mower and cut the grass." Then she went back to what she was doing. She probably didn't give it a second thought. But that was a turning point in MY life.

I had my target, my WHY. Now, sometimes that target moved, and I had to adjust. But I kept my eyes on it at all times.

When you're chasing your rabbit, there has to be a consistency to the chase. You can never forget the big picture. The whole thing must be bigger than you. Even when you have the trials and tribulations of life, even when you get knocked off your perch by some setback, that bigger goal DOESN'T EVER CHANGE. You never let it change. Your eyes should be fixated on it.

When dogs are chasing their rabbit, it's all about the hunt. It's very primitive, almost like a survival instinct that probably has existed since the beginning of time. When you're chasing your rabbit, it's going to be a lot more thoughtful. How do you discover your why? You need to ask yourself some hard questions.

What are you passionate about? What do you love? What are things you could talk about for hours on end? What really lights you up? What comes naturally to you and what are some things that other people notice about you that maybe bring out some compliments?

You starting to get a clearer picture now?

Once you discover your why—and you start chasing your rabbit—it's like getting a road map for your life's path. If you're passionate about helping people, maybe you're destined to become a social worker. If you're an athlete who loves the game, even though the odds might be against reaching the NFL or NBA, maybe your future is in coaching or working as a sports analyst.

To find your rabbit, focus on your values and goals. Think about what you've learned from your experiences. Then dream a little bit. What do you want to do with your life?

Once you know your why, you'll be unstoppable. Trust me.

That rabbit won't have a chance.

Motivation Makes a Difference

"How's it going today?"

How often do you say that? How often is it said to you?

Some people almost sleepwalk through their responses.

"Yeah, I'm good, I guess."

"Not too bad."

"Oh, I'm making it."

Do these folks sound super-motivated to you? Would you follow them anywhere? Would you expect them to be super-achievers? Are they excited to be alive? I'm telling you, motivation MAKES A DIFFERENCE.

Look, you've got to have something that WAKES YOU UP in the morning. If you know your rabbit, if you know your why, motivation should NOT be a problem.

We all need these goals. I've got to have something that motivates me to get out of bed without an alarm clock. When you have the focus that just makes you want to GO GET IT, there's nothing like that feeling.

One thing, though. Your goal must be BIGGER THAN JUST YOU. Because if it's just about you, we all have that element of quit in us. We have all shut down. If we're pushed hard enough to feel that pressure, we all have that desire to just . . . let . . . go.

If it's about just you, there's a propensity to quit on yourself. The person who jogs alone, if they quit, nobody knows they're quitting but them. But if you're jogging with a friend and you quit, well, that's a LOT different. You're going to feel like you let your friend down. That friend can tell another friend. Then you're known as a quitter.

Work to help a group of folks close to you, like your family or your coworkers. Find a cause that's gonna make your community better. Establish something really cool—like productive activities for kids who need some purpose. Those kinds of things will change those people's lives long after you're gone. When you have folks counting on you, no way you're gonna be stopped until you achieve your mission.

If you're motivated beyond belief, I'll tell you this right now, you WILL NOT quit.

That's why the right kind of motivation goes hand in hand with your rabbit and your why. It's the fuel that gets your motor going.

See, one of the biggest misconceptions about me was that my career and accomplishments were ALWAYS about me. If people take a closer look, they'll see that it was NEVER about me. My motivation to chase that rabbit—taking care of my mama and now taking care of my kids—was always WAY bigger than any personal thing.

Some people are just wired to be highly motivated. They are the folks who live by the saying "Never say never."

They DO NOT give up—ever—and they are constantly pushing beyond their comfort zone. They are internally driven, and they don't waste their time judging other people or spreading gossip. They are REAL PEOPLE. I love it.

For others, finding motivation can be a struggle. So how can you learn how to develop that PASSION and BURNING DESIRE to always succeed?

It's HARD to stay motivated all the time. I'll admit that. To help, you need some SPECIFIC goals. And you should always surround yourself with positive people. Those are two big steps to set up the right mindset, where you automatically feel that urgency to chase your rabbit.

If you just aren't feeling it, if you aren't waking up roaring like a tiger, I've got a few things that can help. Try breaking down your goals into smaller, more manageable steps so they won't seem like a mountain that you just can't climb. Don't get down if you have a setback. That's part of the journey. Lean on the people who care about you, the ones who want your success.

And even if you have a SMALL accomplishment along the way, give yourself a REWARD. Trying to lose twenty pounds? When you get to five, find a way to treat yourself (but NOT with a piece of chocolate cake, y'all!). Make half your sales for the month? Go take part of the next day off and head to a movie, preferably one that's pure escape.

When you break it down into attainable goals, each time you accomplish one of them, it's gonna keep your motivation going strong and will keep you plowing through them. If you got that kind of motor, you'll do big things.

Vision Quest

If you're a highly motivated person, if you're focused on the why, if you're constantly chasing your rabbit, I can guarantee you one thing:

You have a VISION.

The Bible says, "Where there is no vision, the people perish." That confirms what we already know. It's possible to work like crazy and spin yourself into the ground.

Without vision, we wander around aimlessly. Without vision, our MOTIVATION and our WHY never get off the ground.

Anybody can believe in something they can see and touch. It takes a special person to trust in something they can't yet see. Many people would've laughed at the seven-year-old me who claimed he was one day going to make enough money to retire his mama. But I BELIEVED. Nobody was telling me any different.

That's the kind of VISION—the kind of BELIEF—that puts your life over the top.

If you're a bartender working in the back of the restaurant, you need to see a way to OWN that restaurant. And if you already own that restaurant, why not own multiple restaurants? You always gotta be striving.

If you're caught up in the day-to-day struggle, maybe you don't feel you have the vision for something bigger. Here's where I think a positive attitude makes all the difference.

Everybody has a dream, but many people don't share it because they fear being ridiculed by their friends. That doesn't make the dream any less real or important. But if you don't have any CONFIDENCE—if the possibility of FAILING has got you stopped in your tracks—that dream is gonna stay a dream and nothing more. When you speak your dream into existence, not only does it become more real, but you might come across other folks who can SEE IT or maybe help get you going. That's what having a vision is all about. And don't be afraid to tap into somebody else's vision, too.

There's sometimes a very fine line between somebody who finds their dream and somebody who loses everything. What are those things that cause us to lose sight? Bad choices. Wrong decisions. Selfishness. Stubbornness. Arrogance. All those things that will eventually catch up to you and make you pay a price.

If your attitude blurs your vision, that will be like when it rains. The consistency of rain can be very frustrating, and it can also be very beautiful. Just like the rains of life, it's going to be determined by the way you see it.

The thing about rain sometimes is the way it makes people so upset. All they see are the things they CAN'T DO because there's inclement weather. But the farmer is happy. Oh yes, the farmer is very happy. The guy who owns the lake is happy. The grass is going to be green. The lake will be replenished. And things will grow. It's a COMPLETELY DIFFERENT OUTCOME when you visualize it differently.

That's why I say I don't have BAD DAYS. While I may have a BAD MOMENT, I don't have bad days, because whatever it is that is challenging me, I can see it differently and understand the good that can happen in what is often perceived as a bad situation.

When you have bad eyesight, they give you glasses and suddenly everything comes into focus. But what do you need to do to correct the other kind of bad vision?

Mostly, you need to understand your values. Once you do that, you're going to have a vision for your future. What kind of life do you want to live? What kind of impact do you want to have on the world?

Once you have a vision, it's time to TAKE ACTION.

Don't go waiting for the perfect moment because the moment will NEVER be perfect. Just start taking some steps in the direction of your dreams. The more action you take, the clearer your vision will be. And that will give you the motivation to keep going.

Motivating Others

Some folks know what their rabbit is. Others don't have a clue. They want to do good. They really do. But they just don't know how to get started or they can't even move without being pushed a little bit.

Maybe I'm describing somebody you work with. Or maybe this sounds like one of your kids. You already know that people don't work at the same rate, and they're often motivated by different things.

So, if you're the boss—or the head of a family—how can you get your folks moving in a positive direction?

Get to know them better.

You heard me.

Get to know them better.

Even if that means someone you've known most of your life, like a child, a sister, or a spouse. That means talking to them on a real level, getting to know their hopes and dreams.

When you interact with people, you start to pick up on their hot buttons, what really gets them going. The answer is probably going to be different for each person. That personal connection is going to serve you well. If people feel like you value them and you listen to their ideas, they will be more likely to work hard for you.

That's a start.

You must be transparent—all the time. If it's a business decision or a way you're choosing to operate, if you don't share that information EFFECTIVELY and IMMEDIATELY, your folks will draw their own conclusions. You're looking for their buy-in, so you can't allow an atmosphere where they're guessing or feeling like they've been kept in the dark.

When it comes to my players—and young people in general, really—they want to know WHY something is being asked of them. They also want to feel like they've got ownership of their situation and they're not being micromanaged to death. If they don't have a good feel for the WHY, they're NOT going to do it. It's that simple.

Not everybody is a good candidate for advancement and not everybody can get everything they want. But if they feel like they've got a fair shot at getting to a higher position with higher pay, that might be their biggest rabbit right there.

Give your folks some incentive. If there's a monthly bonus for the person with the highest sales figures or extra time off for everybody if certain goals are reached, that's a win-win.

You need some balance in all of this, too. Productivity is one thing, but you gotta avoid burnout. Be sure to be conscious of mental health and always know situations WILL come up, whether it's a family issue or a sick child or parent. So be reasonable and have a heart.

Here's a big one: Don't be afraid to fail. That's true of you and it's true of all your folks. You want them to be creative risk-takers, right? Well, if the plan doesn't work, you can't be all critical and second-guessing or else they will go into a shell. Learn from failure. Don't make the same mistake twice. But don't you default to MEDIOCRE because you're getting gun-shy. Keep going after it.

Your rabbit might not be somebody else's rabbit. But we all need to be chasing something. That's the rhythm of life. That's why we're here. So, if your folks are hesitant, go ahead and help them find their rabbit. Once they find it, trust me, they'll be off and running.

COACH PRIME'S TAKEAWAYS

1. **We're all chasing something. That helps us discover our WHY.** Focusing on your values and goals will lead to your dreams. Once you get those areas clear in your mind, it's time to start the chase!

2. **Find something that's going to get you out of bed without an alarm clock.** That level of self-motivation will make you look forward to every single day and give tremendous PURPOSE to your life.

3. **If you aren't feeling it, try breaking down your goals into smaller, more manageable steps so they won't seem so overwhelming.** Don't get down if you have a setback. That's part of the journey. Even if you have a SMALL accomplishment along the way, give yourself a REWARD.

4. **You can have a bad moment, but don't have any bad DAYS.** You've got to have vision. See it in your mind before it happens. And the more action you take, the clearer your vision will be. Vision is like an unshakable confidence that's going to put your life over the top.

5. **When you're helping other folks find their rabbit, you've got to be transparent and explain WHY something must be done.** Leaders MUST follow through on this. If you can't pinpoint WHY something should be done or the PURPOSE behind your direction, there's a great chance they just aren't going to do what you want them to do.

CHAPTER 14

Open Doors for Others

You know what irritates me? I mean, what REALLY irritates me?

When you see some guy entering a restaurant and there's a lady—or maybe an elderly person—right behind him. The guy opens the door . . . and heads on in!

Excuse me? You're not even thinking about holding that door open for the lady or senior?

What happened to our manners? Yeah, we're living in a me-me-me world and everybody's looking to get theirs. But it's disappointing to see so many people who are oblivious to doing even the little things for others.

Don't get me wrong. The world has lots of wonderful people who are all about helping others, but the fact that your coach needs to even mention this issue is sad in my eyes.

And that's just how it goes with everyday folks. If you have a big platform, you are OBLIGATED to give back in a bigger way. When we got hired at Jackson State, we met with the local pastors one day, then gang leaders, drug dealers, and hood heroes the next day. I'm a godly man. I live by faith and godly principles. I knew that I needed those pastors to help us pray through storms and trials and tribulations. And they were excellent sounding boards for our kids. When you go to the street, that probably seems like a different universe. It's actually the same darn thing, just a different ministry. Their role is just as important. One kid looks up to the pastor. Another kid looks up to the hood hero, the one who runs the neighborhood and regulates things. Some of our kids grew up in that environment, and they don't want to go back, but they understand it.

Our goal was to unite the city, and EVERYBODY had a role in that. There was a homecoming against a rival school that had trouble with violence surrounding the game. We announced at the weekly press conference — "No killin' . . . we chillin'." We wanted to protect our own players, but also promote the right thing to do in the community. As the football coach and one of the leaders in the community, I felt I had to be very visible in practically everything that affected the city.

When you're in the world of college football or athletics in general, it's easy to get lost in your work bubble. You lose sight of the real-life stuff that's going on outside your circle. We've all got to step outside that circle from time to time, look around, learn what people really care about. The world is a lot bigger than any individual, any team, or any school.

We see the goodness of people all the time. When somebody is facing a crisis or a serious illness, you see folks rallying around them, which is great. And it's even greater if they're doing it without looking for attention or credit.

But the little things, like failing to hold open a door for someone? We don't stand for such things in my family or on our team. And this all starts by having compassion for and an awareness of other people.

The longer you live, the more you realize:

It's not about YOU.

It's about what YOU can do for THEM.

The Kindness of a Stranger

Has your life ever been changed in a profound way by someone you DON'T EVEN KNOW? Think about that. All the people in your life—your family, your classmates, your coworkers, everybody in the circle—and then some stranger makes an impact that you'll remember for years. And you don't even know the person's name?

That's wild.

Let me tell you a story.

One day, I was driving home from the Dallas–Fort Worth airport. I saw this gentleman walking on the side of the road, way past the airport, pulling his luggage. Now that's something you don't see every day.

I thought to myself, *What just happened with this guy? What just happened?* I didn't even think that he could be a robber, a murderer, or anything like that. I went through a plethora of things in my mind that could've happened. Maybe his car wouldn't start? Maybe he lost his wallet? Or maybe he was just down on his luck.

Most of us would just think it's odd and keep driving and going about our day, right? Well, I found myself pulling over to the side of the road and asking this guy, "Where do you need to go?" He looked at me in shock, in pure amazement.

The fact that maybe I was a significant person, somebody who might be recognized by others, that has nothing to do with this story. It was purely one person looking to help another person who he knew didn't deserve to be in that situation. Because no one walks along the roads around the airport pulling their luggage unless something has gone really, really wrong.

So, I picked him up, took him to his location, and said, "God bless you," then pulled off and didn't think too much more of it.

I'm a Black man, who didn't know him from Adam, had nothing to gain, probably a lot to lose, maybe my life by pulling over and offering a random stranger a ride. I'm taking a chance. But seeing the kindness of somebody's heart, picking you up in a nice vehicle, thinking you were worthy enough to reach your destination and you didn't deserve the hand you were dealt . . . I'm pretty sure those things crossed his mind as he thought about whether to get in my car.

And let's get straight on this. It wasn't whoever I was. It wasn't the type of car I was driving. I'm pretty sure he didn't have a clue about that. In that moment it was just about having a good heart.

So, what was this man's REAL story? I know y'all are dying to know. The answer is . . . I don't know. I never asked him. His story was not my concern. The only thing that mattered was getting him to his destination.

If you're opening doors for someone at the mall or the shopping center, you're not stopping to ask people about their story. You're just helping them out of common courtesy. You may never see that person again. But in that brief moment, you are being courteous and of assistance to them. To the other person, who may in fact be having a hard day, that small gesture is meaningful. Have no doubt about that.

Too many times we get all involved in someone's story and ask a lot of questions. We get clouded by that stuff, then we find these other factors can cause us not to perform a kind gesture. We get thinking about it and we decide it's not worth it.

I just feel like as a person you should bless others. You don't have to. But you should. I was just raised that way. So that's what I did.

Moving forward, it wasn't the impact on me. It was the impact on him. Because now that gentleman is gonna be in that same situation somewhere in life and he's gonna think about that time a stranger helped him. And when he sees someone less fortunate, he's gonna think, *That was me. And on that day, someone gave me an opportunity.* And so I bet, if he gets the chance, that gentleman will give someone else an opportunity to pay it forward.

We're always busy. Sometimes, we don't feel like we should get involved. But if you take the time to help someone—maybe someone you don't even know—it's amazing how that can continue to help the world. You show a little human kindness to someone and they're liable to do the same thing for the next person.

Giving Opportunity

I vividly remember the first time a stranger reached out to me. It changed my life.

Dave Capel, coach of the Fort Myers Rebels, saw me playing inner-city league football when I was around six years old. He gave me an opportunity to go across town and play for the Rebels, who were better funded with more resources and a higher level of competition. That one moment, that one opportunity, changed my life and opened the door for pretty much everything else. Talk about the power of one moment!

This man saw the gift of this young Black kid. He recognized my talent and knew I could take it to another level in a different setting. He brought me into a realm of professionalism that I had never seen. I had been playing in organizations that lacked organization, that lacked the right structure.

Football is football, but when I started playing for the Rebels I stepped into a completely different world. All my teammates seemingly had parents who OWNED something, like a business or a large home. They were professionals, including the chief of police and a doctor. These were people who had access and opportunity. Things that up until that point I knew little about.

One of the main streets of promise in the city was McGregor Boulevard. Two of my teammates lived on this street, where they had long driveways that rolled up to major homes. Ever since I saw that scene, anybody who knows me knows that most of my homes had long driveways. I always felt like the longer your driveway, the longer your money.

My teammates lived in places with swimming pools. They had tennis courts. I had never seen that. They ate together every night as a family. We NEVER ate together as a family because somebody was always working. My mother would cook and put the food in the oven to be reheated and eaten later when you got home, and then you cleaned up.

Seeing all this changed my life and my perspective. My countenance changed and it gave me vision.

This man, Dave Capel, flew me, my mama and grandma to North Carolina for a bowl game. I'd never flown before. My mama and grandma had never flown before. This was a first for us.

He taught me so many things, but the most important thing he left me with was that my education was my priority. We had to maintain a certain GPA to play. We also didn't lose a game for THREE STRAIGHT YEARS.

Our team in the Fort Myers Rebels organization was called the "Dynomites!" We had thirty-five guys and I was one of just three Black kids. In 1979, we went to the nationals in Atlanta, and we won the championship for all of Pop Warner football.

Coach Capel told me later that he thought I scored about 120 touchdowns in the time I had with him. People used to say that all I had to do was touch the ball and he was gonna get a touchdown. Sometimes, it seemed too easy. They'd hand me the ball and I'd take it to the house. Coach Capel always said he was grateful to be able to coach a player like me.

Whatever Coach Capel thought I gave to him, he and his teams gave me so much more. It was unbelievable what I learned, what I gleaned, by being exposed to the professionalism, the class, the organization, the relationships with my teammates. When we won the national championship, our team had a combined A-minus *average.* So, he did a lot more than teach us how to play football.

He set all of us on the path to a successful life, on and off the field. He gave me an opportunity.

Coach Capel had three kids of his own—a daughter and two sons—and he always made me feel like I was his third son. Every bowl game I ever played in with Florida State, I gave him a jersey and the towels I wore in the game. This man, Dave Capel, and his wife, Helen, these were my people. I got them tickets to all my bowl games. I got them tickets to the Super Bowls I played in. It was never something they expected, but it was certainly appreciated.

Everything they taught me was the basis of my TRUTH youth organization I started in Dallas. I copied and emulated everything, spun it forward, and did my best to give opportunities to a lot of young people.

Lives were changed by finding a way forward. So much good came from it all. And it all began when a man felt moved to give an opportunity to a kid.

We live in a world where people are constantly giving back and looking to collect on that. We KNOW this because we SEE it all the time. There's always a photo of somebody or some group giving out one of those oversized checks—and that's great. But attention can't be the primary reason you give something back.

The next generation is facing challenges like never before. They need US to set an example. And part of what we must teach them is to always give back, always pay it forward, but with no expectations of getting publicity, praise, or anything other than the knowledge that we did the right thing. If WE do it that way, THEY are going to do it that way. I played for the New York Yankees when George Steinbrenner owned the team. He did so much to help people— and no one ever knew anything about it. He was always sending money to help people he read or heard about who were struggling and in need. Back in Tampa, where he lived, he read a *Tampa Tribune* story about how high school coaches were leaving the profession because their pay was so low. So, to give them some incentive, he started this annual event—they even called it "The Coaches Prom"—where there was an orchestra and dancing and giveaways of trips and a new car. All the coaches dressed up and were made to feel so special. He wasn't doing it for the publicity or notoriety. It was all based on him caring about keeping the coaches engaged and interested in helping the kids. Mr. Steinbrenner always said if more than two people know what you're doing for somebody, it's not really charity.

Here's the thing: Giving isn't something exclusive to just the folks who have lots of money. Giving is a way of life, a sign of character and caring. If you open a door for somebody, if you have a kind word, if you just LISTEN to somebody in need, that's giving.

We all need to revolve our lives around giving opportunity—and not expecting anything in return.

What the Door Represents

We started this by talking about the value of opening doors for people. That door can also be what's preventing someone from getting from Point A to Point B—unless somebody opens it for them.

The other person gives you some effort by pushing the door or pulling it open. When the door is opened, you get to move into the next chapter of your life or start the next part of your journey.

But the best part of opening that door is how it shows one person doing something good without any thought of reciprocation.

Everybody wants reciprocation these days. "I'll do this for you, but what are you gonna give me in return?" We could all benefit from more folks living like they used to, by being good neighbors, simply because that was the way you did things.

Back in the day, we used to go across the street and borrow some sugar to turn our corn flakes into Frosted Flakes. We just asked and help was given. It wasn't because they expected to come over to our house the next day and borrow some milk. They just gave us the sugar because that's what good neighbors do.

Here's the other thing about opening that door: Once you're inside, you can open a window. You can't do that from the outside. You've got to go through the door to open the window. And if you know your Bible, you've heard the phrase "Open the windows of heaven."

Does the simple act of opening a door for someone seem like it's even more significant now?

Give Something Back

It's great to see so many sports teams and business leaders who get involved in their community and support the important causes.

As business leaders, you have a responsibility to more than just your shareholders. Of course, you have obligations to your employees and customers, but you also need to be part of your community.

It ain't just about the money. Some of us believed that when we were younger, but it's funny how time and experiences give you wisdom and the ability to do the right thing. It's about making a difference.

In any venture that you're a part of, you should make it your PERSONAL MISSION to give back in a variety of ways. In my eyes, the business leaders, community leaders, and people of influence who do that are the real MVPs.

When you're the leader or boss, even though you may not realize it, folks are looking at you all the time, listening to what you say, seeing how you react. If you use that platform to help people or raise awareness for important issues, that's a signal for other people to do the same.

I encourage you to speak out against injustice and inequality. I

encourage you to use your influence to effect change. And by helping to support local organizations that do great work in the community, you automatically make a statement that others will notice.

At the end of the day it's about acting and making a difference,
whether it's volunteering at a local food bank, mentoring a young
person, or getting involved in a political campaign.

Now, some people might say that business leaders don't have
time for these kinds of things. They're too busy running their
companies and making money. That's just not true. And it applies
to everyone, whether you own a business or not. All of us should
look to give back.

You've got to make it a PRIORITY. Here's the thing: When
you do give back, it's not just good for the community, it's good for
your business, too. You look at the studies on this and they show
that companies involved in giving back to their communities and
supporting causes have higher employee satisfaction, increased
customer loyalty, and better overall brand perception.

That's right. Giving back is GOOD FOR BUSINESS.

So, find a cause you're passionate about, then put your time
and resources behind it. It's not just the RIGHT thing to do. It's the
SMART thing to do.

And to the rest of y'all, you support those business leaders who
are making a difference. Patronize their businesses. Buy their prod-
ucts. Let them know you appreciate their commitment to the community.

COACH PRIME'S TAKEAWAYS

1. **Life isn't about YOU. It's about what YOU can do for OTHERS.** So be nice to folks. Offer to help them. Build a nice résumé of good deeds for others. Keep it your little secret.

2. **Never underestimate the power of helping someone in need.** You just SET A GOOD EXAMPLE. Maybe that person will now pay it forward and help somebody else. In a small but very significant way, you just changed the world.

3. **Get involved with people. Put them in a position to succeed.** Sometimes, all a person really needs is an OPPORTUNITY, not a handout.

4. **We all need to make a living, but you and your company should stand for more than just profit.** Get involved in your community. GIVE SOMETHING BACK. That will come back to you in ways you'd never expect.

5. **All your athletic trophies, material possessions, job promotions, and business awards will fade in time.** What really lasts are the doors you open for others. That's how you can measure your TRUE IMPACT.

CHAPTER 15

Keep the Main Thing the Main Thing

The main thing is to keep the main thing the main thing."

While I wish I could take credit for this phrase, it was Stephen Covey, author of *7 Habits of Highly Effective People*, who came up with it. It's brilliant, really. And I wholeheartedly agree with all that it means. We hear so much about the importance of MULTITASKING and being ULTRA-PRODUCTIVE. It's almost like we're made to feel guilty if we're not doing ten things at once. I argue nothing could be less true.

You've got to keep the main thing the main thing. You've got to keep your focus and efforts on the MOST IMPORTANT goals, and that will help you accomplish them.

Would you ignore the top account at your business to concentrate on something that's bringing in just a few bucks? Would you stop selling your top item to push a product that had no traction? Or let me cut to the chase for some of you: Would you put the needs of your family on hold in order to climb the corporate ladder? Ouch. That last one might hurt some of y'all.

No matter how crazy life gets, you can't get sidetracked by the stuff that just doesn't matter as much.

Let's say you got a bunch of different tasks to accomplish this week. How do you stay focused on the main thing?

First of all, it's really helpful to make a list. That way you aren't forgetting anything. Crossing things off one at a time as you get stuff done gives you a feeling of accomplishment, which in turn MOTIVATES you to keep crossing things off until everything is done.

Now put your list in order—from the most important to the least important. Not all tasks are created equal, as y'all know. While it may be easier, it's SILLY to spend time on the little things and leave the important stuff undone. It's always good to tackle the biggest thing first. Don't just sit there and stare at it. Break it down into smaller pieces if you need to. But get moving and DO SOMETHING. Once you start, it's not going to seem half as big.

I'm sure y'all have meetings at your work. Maybe too many meetings. I've seen some places where all they do is go from meeting to meeting—except when they break for lunch, of course. Nothing against having a good plan, but you DO have to ACTUALLY WORK on things, instead of just planning and talking about them.

Sometimes there isn't enough time in the day to get everything done. It's frustrating to know there are still things left on your to-do list that you couldn't get to. But if you keep the main thing the main thing, you'll get all the important stuff accomplished. Most of the time, you can live with putting off the rest to another day.

Know Your Priorities

What's most important to you? That's a darn IMPORTANT question. Take all the time you need. Because your answer will probably determine the direction of your life, along with your happiness.

Getting in shape? Going back to school? Starting a family? Going for that promotion? Saving for retirement? Helping in your community?

If you ask ten people, you might get ten answers. And all of them are correct. It's a very personal question and everybody has different goals.

Let's say you have four glass balls. Three of them represent fun activities, hobbies, or luxury items. The fourth represents the things that are most important to you. So, you start juggling those glass balls. While you hope it doesn't happen, it really doesn't matter if you drop the first three and they break. But you WON'T drop that fourth one. You'll dive on the ground to catch it. You'll do ANYTHING to preserve the things that are most important to you.

That's what I mean by PRIORITIES.

"Hey, you better get your priorities straight!" You heard that before? It might be addressed to a young person who's not good at managing their time. It might be said to a coworker who's having trouble organizing their workload.

Look, I get it. We all know it's easy to get caught up in the hustle and bustle of everyday life. We're constantly bombarded with messages telling us we need to be more productive, more successful, more accomplished. But here's what they NEVER say: Unless you're Superman, you CAN'T do it all.

That's why it's so important to know your priorities. When you know what's important, you can make decisions that are in line with your values. You can say no to things that aren't important to you and focus on the things that are.

So how do you determine your priorities? Well, that's a question only you can answer. But here are some ideas that might help:

🏈 **What are your VALUES?** — What's really important to you?

- **What are your goals?** — What do you want to ACHIEVE in life?

- **What are your strengths and weaknesses?** — What are you GOOD at? What do you ENJOY doing?

- **What are your resources?** — What kind of time, money, and energy do you have available?

Now, when you put all of that together, it becomes like a math equation. Some things will add to your life — and some might even help you MULTIPLY your opportunities. If you take a class or a workshop that's going to help you reach your career goals, you just added something to your life even though it probably took some sacrifice.

You've really got to watch out for those things that DETRACT from your life. We all enjoy a night out with friends, right? And sometimes we NEED that social interaction and escape. But use your judgment. Sometimes you have to say no. If a night out will cause you to miss your workout — and get you out of your routine — or put you behind at work, it's best to skip the fun this time and not put yourself in a bad spot.

If you answer all the questions listed above, things will start to take shape. You can begin a list of priorities, maybe even putting them in order. Now, priorities could change over time — and they probably will — but it's always good to start with a general idea of what's important to you so you can make the right decisions.

Once you know your true priorities, you can start living your life accordingly. That means saying NO to things that could be very tempting. And it means saying YES to things that may not pay off immediately, but you know they are the right fit. Even when it seems hard, you need to stay in that lane. It's going to help you in the long run.

When you feel like you want to give in to those temptations, when you feel like there's not possibly enough time to get everything done, you should always keep the BIG PICTURE in mind. That will help you find a way to make it happen.

What are you waiting for? Get those priorities lined up. Then live your life by those rules. I GUARANTEE it's going to be the best decision you'll EVER make.

Staying True to Your Focus

When I was a kid, if I wasn't playing ball, I was probably hanging out with my friends. And there was a pretty good chance that one of us was saying something like, "Man, there's nothing to do!"

We made up games with sticks and rocks if we had to. We looked up at the clouds and said what their shapes reminded us of. We imitated funny voices or noises. Bottom line, we used our IMAGINATION.

Nothing to do? Is that even a thing anymore? If you ask me, there's WAY TOO MUCH to do.

I remember when I was a kid there were three or four TV channels. Now, within seconds, we can watch practically any movie ever made. All the information we could ever dream of—along with dozens of crazy games—is within reach on our phones. Want a new pair of shoes? Just punch a few buttons and they'll be on your doorstep by the next afternoon.

We got a problem, y'all. We got TOO MUCH going on. No wonder our attention spans are so much smaller these days. No wonder some kids have major trouble when it comes to FOCUSING.

We're living in the most amazing time in the history of the world. So why are we complaining? If you ask me, I think we got way too many DISTRACTIONS.

Here's the thing: Tech is a blessing. Tech is meant to help us be efficient. But just like a carpenter or an electrician knows how to use their tools, all of us need to know how to properly use our tech tools so they can help our lives. If we don't use them the right way, they can harm us rather than HELP us.

Distractions are everywhere. They're in our businesses. They're in our lives. Really, they are the ENEMY because they can keep us from achieving our goals.

I don't care if you're a businessperson, a parent, or a professional athlete, you've got to know how to tame those distractions. So how do you stay focused and on track these days?

First thing, you must know your goals. Once you get your goals down, then you can start to IDENTIFY the distractions that stand in the way.

You've got to set some boundaries. If you're a student or a working person, you can't stay out all night. When you're well rested, healthy, and happy, you're better able to focus and resist distractions. It's basic stuff, but you've got to make sure you're getting enough sleep, eating healthy foods, and exercising regularly.

And if you're at work on a project, you can't let your personal life get in the way. By the same token, when you're chilling at home, DON'T be checking your work email or taking work calls unless it's an emergency. Leave your phone in another room if the temptation to check it all the time is too great.

It's a HUGE help to get a support system of friends, family, or colleagues who can help you stay accountable and focused. You can rely on those folks to encourage you when you're feeling down or help you stay on track when you're tempted to give up.

Here are a few more tips that keep distractions out of your life:

- **Be disciplined**—To me, that's the ultimate key. You must say no to things that ARE NOT IMPORTANT.

That's the only way to stay focused on your goals. Use social media for the good instead of making it into a time-waster.

- **Be organized** — Y'all have one of those desks in the office that looks like a complete disaster? It's hard to change those habits of disorganization, but I'm telling you, you GOT to. The cluttered workspace and cluttered mind go together like cheese on grits. Make sure you get a system that lets you organize your work and your thoughts.

- **Take breaks** — Burnout is real, folks. You need some breaks throughout the day. Don't stay planted in that chair, trying to be a workplace hero. Get up. Move around. Stretch those legs. Grab some fresh air. You stay in that chair and get tired, you'll be daydreaming for sure.

- **Reward yourself** — When you reach a goal, give yourself a REWARD. Why not? Make it something you really enjoy. That will keep you motivated and on track.

Don't Major in the Minors

Y'all familiar with Bruce Lee? Man, that cat was amazing. Super-fit, super-quick, super-dangerous with his martial arts. You run into him in a dark alley, you got problems. Not a dude you'd ever want to mess with. I'm mesmerized watching films of how he could operate.

I KNOW you're familiar with Steve Jobs. He was one of the most revolutionary thinkers of our time. He changed our way of life through technology. To know how influential Steve Jobs was, you only have to say one word—iPhone. Yep, discussion over. That guy was WAY ahead of his time.

Bruce Lee and Steve Jobs. What would these guys POSSIBLY have in common?

A lot, actually.

These guys both believed in MINIMALIST living and thinking. They believed that in order to achieve the maximum results, you don't keep adding things to the system. In fact, if something is unnecessary, if it's not adding something positive, you get RID of it—immediately. Don't major in the minors. The little stuff will only bog you down.

As a fighter, Bruce Lee was unique. He would not do moves just for show, like many of his competitors. All his moves had a purpose. He was into FUNDAMENTALS. He was lean and efficient. He was determined to "hack away at the unessential."

You'd think of a technology genius as a detail guy, right? But that wasn't the genius of Steve Jobs. Everybody knows how to use an iPhone or an iPad. If they pick one up for the first time, they could easily figure out how to use it and how to open an app. He made them intuitive. One thing's for sure: Intuitive doesn't work as well if you insist on adding clutter and stuff that just isn't necessary. According to Jobs, "Simple can be harder than complex. You have to work hard to get your thinking clean to make it simple. But it's worth it in the end because once you get there, you can move mountains."

One surefire way to keep the main thing the main thing is to keep it simple. And that will prevent you from majoring in the minors.

What do I mean by keeping it SIMPLE? Here are some ways you can apply that to your daily life:

> **Don't try to do TOO MUCH at once**—It's better to focus on one thing at a time and do it well instead

of trying to do everything and having it all come off halfheartedly.

- **Break down big jobs into smaller, more manageable steps**—It's gonna seem less intimidating and more ACHIEVABLE.

- **Ask for help. If you're struggling, reach out**—There are plenty of people willing to help—especially if you've helped them before.

- **Don't change EVERYTHING overnight**—Think of it as a lifestyle evolution. Make small changes. You going on a diet? Maybe cut out the sugary drinks or eat one less serving of processed food each day. That stuff will add up.

- **Don't try to do everything yourself**—If you're starting a business, hire some EXPERTS in their fields to help with things you don't know how to do. Whatever it costs, it's going to be WELL WORTH IT. Think of it as an investment.

Keep it simple, y'all.
And don't major in the minors.

Don't Let Circumstances Control Your Outcome

Let me tell you a story about a lady who was raised in poverty and sexually abused as a child. She got hired as a television news anchor, but they fired her for being "too emotional" on air. She didn't let that stop her from the life she imagined. She became one of the world's most successful talk-show hosts and a billionaire philanthropist.

Maybe you've heard of OPRAH WINFREY.

Let me tell you about a man who was raised by a single mother. He was surrounded by poverty and street violence. When he began sliding in school, she sent him to live with his basketball coach, who taught him structure and the right priorities. Not only did this kid grow into one of the greatest NBA players of all time, but he created a school in his hometown of Akron, Ohio, a safe, nurturing place that turned around a steep dropout rate. And he continues to support organizations that help children facing hunger, education, water, and health issues.

I know you're familiar with LEBRON JAMES.

There was this other lady who was a single mother living on welfare when she finished her first book. It got rejected by twelve publishers. Other people would've just given up. Not her. Finally, somebody agreed to publish her book and that faith was justified. And, you know, the book did pretty well.

The author's name is J.K. ROWLING. She wrote the *Harry Potter* books, one of the most popular series in publishing history.

All these very famous and accomplished people overcame difficult circumstances to achieve their goals. They didn't let circumstances control their outcome or their destination.

If they did it, why can't YOU? If you work hard, believe in yourself, and never give up on your dreams, you'll be following their path and carving out your own success.

The lesson here is to NEVER ALLOW what's happening around you to dictate how you feel or what you do. Don't let the bad things in life get you down. Don't let the naysayers tell you that you CAN'T do something.

Hey, sometimes that's not easy. I hear ya. But you have to keep going. You have to BELIEVE in yourself. Because as I said before, and I'll say again, if you don't, who will?

Now, there's no such thing as a free lunch. There's not even a reduced lunch in real life. If you want it bad enough, you've got to go out there and get it.

Don't let your past define you. No matter who you are, you've got a past. You've made some mistakes. But don't let that hold you back. Learn from those mistakes and move forward with CONFI-DENCE.

Don't let other people's opinions CONTROL you. As you know, everybody has an OPINION. But that doesn't mean their opinion is RIGHT. Decide what's right for you. If other people have an opinion about it, let them talk—because they WILL talk—but don't let that sway you.

While fear is a natural emotion, you cannot let it get in the way. Deep down, we're all a little scared of something—needles, rats, snakes—but that shouldn't prevent us from doing great things or even just doing what has to get done.

Don't be scared of SUCCESS. That's right. I said it. Don't be scared of SUCCESS. You're as deserving of good things as anyone else. Don't let anybody tell you differently.

And on the flip side, no matter how desperate your situation might SEEM, there's always a way to move forward.

COACH PRIME'S TAKEAWAYS

1. **Don't buy into the illusion of multitasking as the be-all, end-all way of doing business.** Put most of your energy into your most important tasks. Keep the main thing the MAIN thing.

2. **Determine your priorities. Consider your values, goals, strengths, and weaknesses.** Once you know your priorities, you have a road map for your life. In the grand scheme of things, it's not a big deal if you go off track with your hobbies and leisure activities. But PROTECT YOUR PRIORITIES at all costs.

3. **Distractions can knock you off the path to success, so you've got to stay DISCIPLINED and ORGANIZED.** Know your goals like the back of your hand and set some boundaries. If you're taking a 250-mile trip on the interstate to see your best friend, you're not getting off at every exit. Keep your eye on the darn ball.

4. **Keep it simple. If there's clutter in your life that's getting in the way of your progress, get rid of it— immediately.** Use social media to your advantage, not as a time-waster. It seems crazy, but if you take a minimalist approach, that could be the route to MAXIMUM results. Sometimes human beings just try to do too much.

5. **No matter how difficult your situation seems, there's always a way to chase your dreams.** Mix hard work with BELIEF and you're on your way to changing your life.

CHAPTER 16

Fight for What's Right

You ready to fight?

Now, I know some of y'all don't want to hear that word. Seems like we're always fighting these days—between political parties, ethnic groups, countries, and territories. Everybody's yelling at somebody. Everybody's mad at the world.

To break this down, I think we need to define that word . . . "fight."

Back in the day, some of us had to fight at the bus stop just to make sure we got a seat on the bus. We had to fight because somebody said something about our sister or our brother or our mama. Those were FIGHTING WORDS.

We think of some guys slapping or punching each other, maybe rolling around in the grass, as a bunch of others gather around in a circle and start cheering. Or maybe we think of somebody trying to settle things with a weapon.

Fighting is mentioned in the Bible, but not in a way like any of the above. The Good Book talks about the "good fight of faith." The two words I noticed are "good fight," which means the fight could have gone either way.

What are you willing to fight for?

Are you willing to fight for what's right and stand up? Or lower your head and look away?

A "fight" doesn't have to be a heat-of-the-moment thing or a physical altercation. It can mean choosing to stand up for someone who needs your support. It can mean never giving up on your co-workers or teammates. It can mean standing up to oppression and working to get out of poverty. In some countries, you're constantly fighting for your freedom.

The funny thing about fighting is that sometimes you get hurt more when you choose *not* to fight. If you just give up, if you just quit, that's a whole lot worse than failing.

We live in a world where people play the political game, always worried about what others think. Sometimes, they refuse to even give an opinion unless they know which way the majority is leaning. They're more concerned about fallout from negative comments on their social media instead of standing up strong and pushing back on an injustice.

I will PROMISE you this: You'll never feel more alive than when you're fighting for something you believe in with all your heart and soul. And if you DON'T fight for it, that moment will haunt you because you'll always know that you weren't true to yourself.

Don't be upset because you've got enemies. That's a badge of honor. If you have enemies, first and foremost, that means you're headed in the right direction. It also means you've stood up for something important. You want to have nothing but friends? Just nod your head and agree with everyone? Never stand up for anything? Sure, everybody might love you then. But they won't RESPECT you.

Too many people do what's easy. I ask you—no, I BEG you—to always do what you think is right, even if it's hard or unpopular.

Dealing with Conflict

All fights have their roots in some sort of conflict. Call it what you want: A disagreement. A difference of opinion. It might be a long-term grudge. Sometimes it's a rivalry. Maybe it's two people going for the same boyfriend or girlfriend. "All's fair in love and war," as the saying goes.

There are some people out there who ENJOY conflict. They seem like they live for it. Some bosses believe it's healthy to have it as part of the job. But most of the world is not down with it. They'd prefer to get along and have a happy life instead of always arguing about something.

WE SPEND MOST OF OUR TIME AT WORK OR AT HOME, SO IT MAKES SENSE THAT THOSE ARE THE TWO PLACES WHERE WE HAVE THE MOST CONFLICT IN OUR LIVES. Conflict can often be bubbling here, near the surface.

So how do we deal with this type of conflict? You don't need boxing gloves, but you DO need some common sense. Navigating conflict is not easy, but you must acknowledge it and you have to know how to keep things settled down in order to have peace in your life.

I know y'all love your family. But let's be REAL. Sometimes your family can get on your last nerve. That's just a fact of life. Nobody can make you MORE UPSET than the people you love the most, whether it's your spouse, your kids, or your parents. They just seem to know the right buttons to push to set you off.

The best thing you can do to keep things at a calm and respectful level is communicate. Y'all need to TALK TO EACH OTHER. I don't mean yelling and screaming. I'm talking about having a real conversation. That means talking—and listening. It's important to listen to each other, let each side have their say, and understand where everyone is coming from.

I've heard some horrible stories about arguments in a family where one person refuses to take back the vicious words they've said, and as a result, the relationship between the two people is never the same. Sometimes, they stop talking altogether or maybe they're never together in a room again. That's no way for blood kin to act. Sometimes, you need to put that pride aside. Sometimes, winning a fight just isn't worth it.

If it gets that bad in a family, I suggest FORGETTING about who's the winner and who's the loser in the argument. It ain't about WHO'S RIGHT. It's about DOING THE RIGHT THING. Put down your swords. Get to the table and do some talking.

To get the conversation going, you need to acknowledge that it's OK to agree to disagree. You won't always see things the same way. That's true in ANY family. But that doesn't mean you can't love and respect each other.

If things get too heated, take a break. Step away and cool off before coming back and continuing to talk things through. These are things you can do with the kids as well. Kids are always fighting, right? The funny thing is kids probably have the BEST sense of family. Even if they're fighting with their brother or sister, nothing gets them in a fighting mood more than SOMEBODY ELSE picking on their sibling. That shows you they know their true colors. Family is family.

Navigating conflict in the workplace can be a little trickier as you're dealing with people you probably don't know as well as family. But one thing remains the same—communication is key. If you have an issue with a coworker or your boss, don't just SIT THERE and stew about it. Doesn't it drive you crazy to have someone complaining and talking behind your back, then when you confront them, they say, "Oh everything is fine." But it's NOT fine.

Some folks just don't want to stir anything up. But you can't get anything solved that way. So, if you have an issue with somebody at your workplace, you need to talk to them. Be honest. Explain what the problem is and how it's affecting you. Once again, you need to listen to what the other person has to say.

Here's the real difference-maker for me. It's very important to keep it PROFESSIONAL. Don't let emotions get the best of you. Don't turn it into a game of name-calling and start dredging up things that aren't even part of the issue. Stay calm, focused, and on point. And if things get really bad, don't be afraid to bring in a third party, like a supervisor or an HR representative. Sometimes it's easier to have an impartial person mediate the situation.

Besides work and home, sometimes the biggest space for conflict can be IN YOUR OWN HEAD. And that might be the toughest of all kinds of conflict. Because oftentimes, we're our own worst enemy. We can't help ourselves and we keep falling into the same thought patterns.

In those instances, it's usually good to take a break from the situation and do something you really enjoy. Go for a walk or a bike ride, watch a movie, spend time playing with your kids. You gotta take care of yourself. Conflict might be a part of life—even when it's a conflict within yourself—but it doesn't have to be something that tears us all apart.

Remember that communication, respect, and some patience can help you work through these conflicts and come out even stronger on the other side. Sometimes a little friction can help bring people together. But you gotta approach it the right way and always keep the big picture in mind.

Fighting Against the Bad Guys

When I was a kid, I used to love watching cartoons about superheroes. They were always going against the villains and crooks. Nobody rooted for the bad guys.

So, if there are bad guys in your world, you should feel the same way when it comes to standing up for what you believe is right. You've got to make your voice heard in the fight against injustice of any sort.

When it comes to issues like that, you want to be on the right side of history, so it's no time to be meek or quiet. When it matters the most, we need more vocal people in this world.

If you keep quiet when somebody is doing obvious WRONG, that can be perceived as you AGREEING with that wrongdoing. Some people look up to you. If you don't stand up against it, they won't stand up against it either. See how it happens?

We've all seen what's happening in this world. Everybody gets treated unfairly—regardless of ethnicity, social status, religion, and sexual preference—and it's just not right. We've got to back up those folks who can't speak for themselves. You've got to stand and fight for what you believe in.

It's not always an easy path to walk, but it's a necessary one. Whether it's racism, sexism, or any other kind of injustice, we need to rise up and make our voices heard. We can still make a difference. Doesn't matter if you're rich or poor, Black or white. The change starts with one person—and YOU can be that person.

You know how this works. It's like a ripple effect, where one person stands up, and then another, and then another. Before you know it, you've got a movement on your hands. Show me somebody who's taking a stand and I'll show you a LEADER. When you make a solid decision like that, people will follow you.

You can inspire others to take action and create positive change. There might be times when you feel like you're on an island, all alone, and you want to throw in the towel, but you've got to remember why you're doing it. You've got to think about all the lives you're going to impact by standing up for what's right.

There are VERY FEW things more powerful than a group of

people coming together and fighting for what they believe in. We've seen it throughout history with the civil rights movement and the women's liberation movement. When people come together, they can change the world.

So, if you see something that's not right, don't just ignore it. Speak up. Use your voice. Let people know how you feel. And don't be afraid to take action, whether it's protesting, signing petitions, or just having tough conversations with people. Every little bit counts.

Life is not fair. The world is challenging. And we're learning how to deal with it daily. If you're feeling discouraged, remember that you're not the only one who feels that way. There are people out there right now who are fighting for what's right. You may never know their names, but you might benefit from the fight they have experienced.

Don't let the bad guys win!

Picking the Right Spots

Sometimes you've got to pick your spots. There's no shame in walking away if the situation becomes counterproductive. You should always stand up for yourself and be ready to fight for what's right. But most importantly, you need to make the right decisions.

When you're an NFL player and you decide to go out after a game, you find yourself surrounded by all kinds of people. Who are they? What are their intentions? Where is the fake tough guy who's looking to pick a fight and make a name for himself?

Here's what I learned when that would happen: Don't worry about what people say to you. Half the time people are just saying things to push your buttons and get a reaction. I don't bother having conversations with fools. I won't waste my time that way. The greatest gift I've ever possessed is knowing when it's time to walk away. If the situation has no upside, you just walk away.

My second year in the NFL, we were at the Super Bowl in Minnesota. I'm with my guys—Derrick Thomas, Broderick Thomas, and Neil Smith—and we swing into this nightclub. This is Minnesota and it's flat-out *freezing*. We're all wearing mink coats almost down to the floor.

Now, you've got to understand that Derrick went fourth, I went fifth, and Brod went sixth in the same draft. Neil Smith went second the year before that. So, this was a group of some notable players and everyone that night looked like MONEY. And there was the group of dudes that kept circling us, no doubt looking to start something. I've got my eye on them. I've always been able to see the room.

I look at Neil and say, "Dawg, what man do you respect the most in the NFL?"

"Reggie White."

So I say, "You think Reggie White would be here right now?"

Neil just laughs and says, "Come on, man. No way!"

I'm not laughing at all. "Then why are WE here? Because this thing is getting ready to go down in a minute. These cats are sizing us up, man. They're probably calling some more people to show up and they're going to rob us."

Was it worth staying there and fighting those guys, maybe doing the wrong thing at the wrong time? Absolutely not.

We got out of there. We had the ability to walk away and we did. Sometimes you've got to learn how to walk away. Everything isn't meant to be a battle or a confrontation, especially when you're challenged by people with nothing to lose and everything to gain.

Now, it might go against your instincts, but you've got to realize when a situation just isn't right.

You might face some criticism. But if you're smart, you'll realize that you shouldn't let things escalate. You've got to let go and walk away. When everybody sees how it plays out, they'll look back and say you made an intelligent decision.

Knowing when NOT to fight can make all the difference.

Let's Get Physical

When you're in the military or on the police force, you are sometimes required to subdue your subject with hand-to-hand combat. In the ancient Olympics, the wrestlers sometimes fought to the DEATH. And like we talked about before, when you're a kid on the school playground, you might need to fight, just to prove yourself or stop the bully from picking on you.

On the football practice field, we get the occasional fight between a couple of players. It's usually fine after they get their aggression out.

Now, I'm not saying y'all will come to blows in the boardroom or your workplace. I'm not predicting an all-out brawl in the neighborhood cul-de-sac. But here's what I will say: If you had to defend yourself physically, could you do it?

I don't want to scare anybody, but we're living in crazy times, whether it's a mugging, a home invasion, a violent altercation, or even road rage. Staying in good physical shape is a MUST to help remain in control of your situation.

When you're in good shape, not only are you more physically capable of defending yourself but you're also mentally tougher and a lot more confident. That confidence can be the difference between backing down and standing up for yourself.

So how do you get in good shape? This applies to everybody. If you're grinding at work all the time, it's real easy to zone out and head straight for the couch once you get home. DON'T DO IT! I'm not saying you need to be a world-class athlete—like Coach Prime in his PRIME—but you need to get out and move your body around. That's essential.

That means doing things like running, cycling, lifting weights, or even just going out for a brisk walk around the neighborhood. If you want to take it to another level and really build your physical confidence, sign up for some martial arts or self-defense classes. That's where you'll learn how to block an attack, throw a punch or a kick, and how to evade an aggressor. It's also a great workout that gives you a sense of community and support.

Look now, staying in good shape isn't just about your physical fitness. You need to be smart. You've got to be aware of your surroundings and you need a plan for when trouble arises.

This sounds like common sense, but you better be vigilant when you're out and about. You better avoid dangerous areas and situations. Most importantly, you better KNOW how to respond if someone tries to hurt you.

I'm guessing that getting in a fight won't be your choice on a given day. But it pays to be prepared for the unexpected. You want to be able to fight for what's right—and sometimes that means defending yourself and the ones you love.

COACH PRIME'S TAKEAWAYS

1. **You've got to fight for what you KNOW is right.** A "fight" doesn't have to be a heat-of-the-moment thing or a physical altercation. It can mean choosing to stand up for someone who needs your support. It can mean never giving up on your coworkers or teammates. It can mean standing up to oppression and injustice.

2. **If you choose NOT to fight at the moment of truth, if you put your head down because you don't want to get involved, that decision will HAUNT you.** When you're fighting for what's right, you're never going to feel more alive than at that moment.

3. **Conflict is EVERYWHERE these days—in the workplace, within your family, sometimes in your own head.** The key to resolving it is honest communication—and honest LISTENING—while always keeping things respectful and/or professional.

4. **Be on the right side of history.** Don't let the bad guys win. Don't be meek when something is wrong. Stand up for what is right and make sure other people join that fight. You get a committed group of people coming together for a cause, you can CHANGE the world.

5. **Most people won't be looking for a fight in their workplace or out in public. But if the fight comes to you—and the safety of you and your loved ones is at stake—you need to be prepared.** That means staying

in GOOD physical shape. Don't take the easy way out. After work, start a regimen of running, cycling, walking, or working out with weights. The physical conditioning will make you mentally sharp and confident. It's also great to take some martial arts or self-defense classes. Hopefully, you'll never have to get physical with somebody. But if you're forced into a challenging situation, you'll be PREPARED.

CHAPTER 17

Dream Big!

I love to dream.

Now hear me: Dreams aren't some fairy-tale, make-believe nonsense. Dreams are what FUEL us, what INSPIRE us, what make us STRIVE FOR GREATNESS.

So please, by all means, DREAM!

But don't go dreaming AVERAGE. If your DREAM ISN'T BIGGER THAN YOU, there's a PROBLEM with your dream.

There's no dream too big, too wild, too crazy to achieve. And I'm not just talking about becoming a superstar athlete. No, I'm talking about whatever your heart desires, whether it's building your own business, becoming a musician, or even taking a trip to every cool place you've ever imagined in this great big world.

You want to be a doctor? A teacher? An artist? You want to be a parent who raises their kids right? You can do it! You just need to have that dream, that passion, that determination.

Don't be afraid to dream BIG, y'all. There's no limit to what you can achieve if you put your mind to it. Look at what we're doing with technology these days. I mean, who would've thought all our modern conveniences were even possible back in the day? But somebody had that dream, that vision, and they made it happen.

See what I'm saying? You MAKE your dreams happen, too.

Don't you ever give up on them. And don't you doubt what you can achieve. Life is too short to settle for mediocrity. So go all in and chase that dream until it becomes reality.

When you DO achieve that dream? LISTEN. DO NOT forget WHAT you came from. Use your success to inspire, motivate, and encourage others.

You can achieve whatever you want. You just need to have the right mindset and stop listening to all those folks who want to shoot holes in your dream.

I wasn't always Coach Prime. Back in the day, I was just another kid with a dream, a kid who grew up in the Jones Walker Apartments. I was surrounded by a lot of people who were going nowhere fast.

My biggest dream was to retire my mom. As I got more involved in sports, I wanted to CHANGE the game with a whole new level of style and swagger, on and off the field.

Man, there were some SERIOUS doubters out there. Now you call them haters. Where would I be now if I had listened to them? There were people who thought I was all mouth and no game. I took a LOT of pleasure in proving those people wrong.

When I was coming up, there wasn't YouTube or Instagram to showcase my skills. But you know what I did have? My imagination, of course. My dream, too. And a superior WORK ETHIC. Yeah, get that straight right now. Dreams require some work.

I didn't let anybody tell me what I couldn't do. So don't let anybody tell YOU about how to define your dreams. Like they say, if you can dream it, you can do it.

Once I found the route to big-time football, I was RELENTLESS. Nothing was going to stop me. I studied film. I hit the gym. I practiced my craft until it was flawless. And you know what? I became the best darn cornerback in the NFL. Shoot, a lot of people think I became one of the greatest athletes of all time — period.

But it wasn't just about the fame and the money and the jewelry and the fancy cars. It was about LIVING my dream. Now I'm a coach and it's about INSPIRING OTHERS to make their own dreams happen.

If you own a business, if you're the boss, that's your role, too. Don't have your people settle for AVERAGE. Teach them how to be GREAT. Encourage them to dream. Even better, encourage them to ACT on those dreams. Because a dream ain't worth nothing without ACTION.

When I was a kid, I was FOCUSED. I believed that anything was possible if I worked hard and believed in myself. Let me tell you something, it's not just kid stuff. That mindset applies to ANYTHING and EVERYTHING in life.

That's what it's all about. Dreaming big. Achieving your dreams. Then using those dreams to change the world for the better.

You're going to hear from people who say, "All you do is dream, dream, dream. Sooner or later, you gotta wake up and go get it." Now, here's the deal you should tell them:

Should you understand reality?

Yes, of course. But by no means should you be *satisfied* with it.

So, take your biggest desires and dream them into existence. I'm not talking about a magic formula. Your dream needs a clear vision. You've got to believe in yourself, no matter what other people say. Then you take action and you don't give up when it comes to making that dream a reality.

Funny thing is, I don't dream when I'm asleep. I dream when I'm wide awake. I DON'T DREAM WHEN I'M ASLEEP. I DREAM WHEN I'M WIDE AWAKE. That wasn't a misprint. I wanted you to feel that twice.

Here's the difference. I can see it, I can feel it, I can touch it. And I know I can HAVE IT when I see it like that.

I know everyone doesn't have my level of belief or optimism.

Maybe your desires have been crushed right before your eyes and you're having issues believing in anything right now. I don't understand why anyone would be skeptical of chasing your dreams. I chase mine, and I just happen to be really fast.

Do this for me, y'all. And I don't expect this to happen overnight or anything. But the first thing that has to happen is you've got to build back your trust. That's going to take patience, faith, and one step at a time. Put effort into focusing on the good things. If you spend time in nature—it's good for ALL of us to know there are things much bigger than ourselves—and get around some folks who share your beliefs, I think that's going to help point you in the right direction.

No matter what, don't give up on these dreams.

Believe in Yourself

Here's a fun fact: Next to the Bible, my all-time favorite book is *The Little Engine That Could*. I read that story so many times as a kid, I know it by heart.

A couple of trains passed on that engine until he started saying to himself: "I think I can. I think I can. I think I can." And that's what I modeled my career after. That's the mentality I always wanted.

It's the story of an underdog that reaches some difficult goals. Pulling that train over the mountain was no easy task.

Nobody believed in that engine, but that engine believed in itself. That engine said, "I think I can. I think I can." Last time I checked, there was an "I" in the middle of W-I-N. There was an "I" in the middle of D-E-I-O-N. There was an "I" in the middle of P-R-I-M-E. So why wouldn't I have the same thought process of the little engine that could?

I hope you're surrounded by people who believe in you every

day, although I know that might not be the case. Most of us are surrounded by skepticism and negativity. "What makes you think you can do that? Why are you so special? You know you ain't gonna get that, so stop dreaming and get realistic. Come on, man, stay in your lane!"

I'm sure you've heard that negative stuff before, even from the people closest to you.

Now, what happens when you're around folks who believe in you? How do you feel when you get encouragement and compliments? That's right! Your confidence skyrockets. When you surround yourself with other dreamers, your life becomes filled with possibilities, not doubts.

Your mind gets fed a steady diet of belief. That's exactly where you want to be.

That's going to motivate you to ALWAYS believe in yourself, believe in your product, and believe in your dreams. Protect those things with all your might. Those doubters and haters will break you down if you let them. So DON'T YOU LET THEM. Funny how the doubters and haters don't seem to be accomplishing anything, but they are the EXPERTS on what you should be doing.

It's simple, really. Whatever it takes, you've got to believe in yourself. If you don't, how will anybody else believe in you?

The way I was as a player is the way I am as a coach. If you're recruiting against me and we happen to be visiting the same kid on the same night, you better PRAY you get to go first. Because if I go in there, they're going to lock that door and I'm going to get that kid. I will execute that moment and make it mine. And the reason I feel that way is because I BELIEVE IN MYSELF, I believe in my school, and I believe in what we have to offer.

Those are my FACTS OF LIFE. I never doubt ME. I never doubt the gifts God gave me. I never doubt the seriousness and magnitude of the situation. I'm a believer and therefore I feel that God blesses me with the confidence to close a deal and make others believe.

How can YOU get that level of confidence?

You've got to PREPARE like crazy. If you go into a meeting knowing your stuff and having all the answers, that will produce a level of confidence that rubs off on everyone else. It matters how you present yourself and how you speak to people. If you come in stammering, apologizing, and shrugging your shoulders, nobody will believe in what you're trying to sell.

You've got to trust the process. If you've done your homework and you're a sincere person, I GUARANTEE that you're way ahead of the game. Be patient. Never underestimate the ability of a group to simply take the easy way out and agree with the obvious. Give that group something to BELIEVE IN and you'll have everybody nodding and agreeing with you. And once you get that kind of reputation, you'll be the person who gets that automatic respect.

You've got to rise up and meet the moment. When we reflect on our lives, it's really a multitude of moments. What did you do with your moment? Were you ready? Don't get mad at me because I DOMINATED my moment. Every time I get the chance to dominate, I'm grabbing that megaphone, jumping on that stage, and PRODUCING when the lights come on. It's just the way I live my life. So, I suggest you identify the key moments in your life and don't waste them with a mediocre performance. That's very unfulfilling.

That's not you.

Be like that Little Engine.

I think I can. I think I can. I think I can.

Hey, I *know* you can.

Create and Innovate

I already told you about dreaming AVERAGE, remember? I just can't have that. Every dreamer throughout history was doubted, so don't be scared off by your haters. If somebody is laughing at your dream, don't put your head down. You're in GREAT company.

Did you know that Thomas Edison, the man who invented the incandescent light bulb, was unsuccessful a thousand times before he got it to work? When asked how it felt to fail a thousand times, he responded, "The light bulb was an invention with 1,000 steps."

Abraham Lincoln was defeated in seven different elections before he became the sixteenth president of the United States in 1860. He never gave up.

Man, I LOVE that!

I can tell you similar stories about myself. How in my senior year at Florida State we were the preseason number-one-ranked team and we did the "Seminole Rap," a music video where we were just looking to have some fun. But it backfired, and the Miami Hurricanes beat the brakes off us 31–0 in the opener, and we never heard the end of it about that music video. I lost some big games. I struck out with the bases loaded. I had a couple of marriages that didn't work out. I trusted the wrong people and didn't pay attention to the details when our charter school in Texas got shut down.

All those things remind me of the fact that I'm just another guy with flaws, just another guy who makes mistakes. I didn't let any of those things stop me, though. In every case, I tried to use them as a learning experience. I never took my eyes off the bigger picture of what I wanted to accomplish in life.

It tells me—and it should tell YOU—that you never quit on a dream. You keep at it. You keep believing. And what someone else THINKS—particularly the "someone else" who lives a safe life and never takes any risks—should have no influence on how you approach your dream.

Here's another thing. Too many of us want to just blend in. Never be afraid to be DIFFERENT. Don't just check some boxes. Make some HISTORY.

If you're in a meeting and you got an idea, SPEAK UP. I guarantee you somebody else was thinking up an idea but got too scared to raise their hand. Speak up! Separate yourself from the others.

Nothing wrong with being different.

When I was at Florida State in 1987, the Metro Conference championships for baseball and track and field were both being held in Columbia, South Carolina. Well, guess what? I played baseball AND ran track. So, which one was I going to choose? How about . . . both! It started with track. I won the 100- and 200-meter dashes. The next day in baseball, I drove in the winning run when we beat Louisville. The day after that, we were playing Southern Miss in baseball, and I knew there was a chance I couldn't get over to the track for the 4x100 relay. The track coaches were prepared for me not to be available. All of a sudden, after we had just beaten Southern Miss, they told me the Metro track championship was coming down to the final event, the 4x100 relay. Somehow, the timing worked in my favor. So, I ran from the baseball field to the track.

When I got to the track, I still had on my baseball pants. And my baseball teammates were sprinting behind me, so they could check out the race. I ran third and we were behind when I got the baton. Well, I gave it everything I had. I caught the rabbit and we won the 4x100 relay!

We were the Metro track champions!

I wish I could've stayed to celebrate, but we had another baseball game to play. So, it was back to the dugout. I got my baseball uniform back on. I ended up hitting a home run against Cincinnati. We were the Metro baseball champions!

I'm not going to lie. That was one heck of a fun weekend.

When word got out about what happened, people around the country seemed so amazed. Everybody was talking about it—and that was before the Internet. I honestly didn't think it was THAT big a deal because I wanted to do my best to help both teams.

I was blessed with a lot of skills to play different sports. And I loved going from sport to sport. I wish more kids did that today, but everything has been turned into such a big business that they're forced to specialize.

Me? I was good at everything I tried. Maybe I could've played some college basketball because I really hooped in high school. But football was my number one. Or was it baseball? There were definitely times when my baseball didn't take a back seat. Somewhere in there, it occurred to me—maybe I could actually play in the NFL *and* the MLB. I wouldn't have to choose.

I had multiple dreams going at one time. But my biggest dream—the ability to retire my mama—never wavered. Having multiple dreams come true was awesome, but my biggest satisfaction was achieving the overarching dream.

The first chance I had to make money playing sports came when I was drafted by the Kansas City Royals out of high school. I must admit I was tempted by the chance to sign a professional contract and make some money. I knew all about the Royals because they held spring training at Terry Park in Fort Myers.

The manager, Dick Howser, actually talked me out of signing with the Royals because he had heard about my football ability and wanted me to give football the same opportunity I would give baseball. He said, "If we draft you out of high school, we'll draft you out of college."

Sure enough, I got drafted again a few years later, this time by the New York Yankees. I played six weeks of professional baseball—

from Rookie League to Triple-A—over that summer, then returned to FSU for my senior football season.

Just about every versatile athlete puts aside a sport they love to concentrate on the one they think will pay the bills. But I didn't want to give up either sport.

So, there I was going through most of my professional career, playing all the time, usually getting just two weeks off (after the Pro Bowl, right before spring training). That was an insane pace. But that was part of my dream. It wasn't an AVERAGE dream. I was a different cat.

If you're old enough, you might remember my PERSONAL doubleheader in 1992. I played for the Atlanta Falcons in an NFL game in Miami in the afternoon. Then I was taken by private plane to Pittsburgh and suited up for the Atlanta Braves in a National League playoff game against the Pirates.

Quite a feat, right? Not everybody saw it that way. People are always ready to poke holes in your dreams. Ain't that the truth? I was called "selfish," and some people said I was "out for myself." Others called it a "publicity gimmick." Funny, but I didn't hear much talk of that a week later when the Braves won the pennant and I hit .533 in the World Series.

Look, I made the Pro Football Hall of Fame. I was the best cornerback to ever do it. So, there's really nothing to doubt about my football skills. But I also played nine seasons in major league baseball and that was no darn fluke.

I DIDN'T CARE about YOUR opinion because I knew my PURPOSE. My purpose is always tied to my passion. I played two sports because I had a tremendous gift from God, not because I was selfish.

Use that as your example. Dream big. Be different. Don't let people shoot holes through your greatest desires. I could have let people talk me out of achieving these feats. If you listen to folks who tell you, "Oh, be realistic . . . Don't be so foolish," you might be turning your back on your destiny. So don't listen. And follow your heart.

I'm compartmentalized. That's another way of saying I'm super-driven. And that's how you need to be, too. Stick to your goals and dreams. Don't let anybody tell you different.

I can have someone booing and telling me that I'm garbage, and I don't even see them. I'm that locked in. No distractions were permitted in my world. I only allowed people to talk to me about the sport I was currently playing.

You don't have to be playing on national television or become a public figure to have doubters. Y'all know that, right? How many dreams and goals have y'all had shot down right in front of you? You ever been laughed at? Those things HURT, especially if it's your family or close friends who are doubting you. This is where you need thick skin and an unshakable belief in what you can offer this world.

I always understood the gifts that were bestowed upon me. I was dreaming very, very big. I knew I was an innovator, and innovators get criticized and scrutinized. But also, I knew who I was. I was THAT DUDE. I didn't need anybody's validation or a gold jacket to tell me what I could do.

I wasn't playing too many sports to make a statement. I never tried to prove anyone wrong. That was never my motivation. I DON'T CARE about your opinion.

When I look in the mirror, I'm straight. I played both sports because I was GOOD at both sports, not because I was selfish. By doing what I love to do, I'm gonna help your team. Things are always gonna be better by getting the ball in my hand. If you think that's brash or cocky, that's on you. I know I'm speaking the TRUTH.

Most folks dream when they sleep. Sometimes the dream comes to them again when they are wide awake, as déjà vu. I don't do that. I SEE the dream clearly while I'm awake. And then I make it happen.

When I was with the 49ers, we went to Atlanta, and it was my first time playing AGAINST the Falcons. On the flight over, I told everybody I'd get a pick. I'd go down the sideline, high-stepping, and I'm going to look at them when I get one. And that's EXACTLY HOW IT HAPPENED. I was always good at visualizing and manifesting things.

If you believe in your dream enough, it won't matter what the crowd thinks. Be a different cat. And never let nobody steal that dream.

Dream a Bigger Dream

Don't dream average. Dream BIG. Don't just maintain. INNOVATE and SEPARATE yourself from the others. Do it in a way it has never been done before. Don't settle for getting by. Leave it much better than you found it. Make it where people will admire your handiwork and know that your efforts were truly SPECIAL.

You don't like the way something looks? Well, change the landscape.

The world will belong to the folks with the new ideas, not the ones who grind the old ideas into the ground in the name of "tradition." Now I like tradition and loyalty as much as anyone, but I also believe in changing with the times and staying current. If you do that, you get ELEVATED. If you don't, you get TERMINATED. That's just the way things work in business, whether it's the business of coaching, running a store, or opening a restaurant.

I have a dream. A brand-new dream.

I would like to become the first Black coach to win a national championship in major college football.

We're GONNA get that done at Colorado. Championships are wonderful. That's our goal. That's what we're chasing. But we're also chasing SIGNIFICANCE. We want our program to

stand for something great. We want to CHANGE THE LAND-
SCAPE.

We took some criticism over how active we were in the transfer portal. When we took over at Colorado, I laid it out loud and clear. I told everyone, "It's my job to find replacements for each of you. It's YOUR JOB not to let me." We talked to twenty players about how tough it was gonna be. The rest of them quit on their own. We got blamed for people quitting on their dream, and the general public said we were cruel. No, we were HONEST.

We knew the type of players we needed to turn around Colorado. So, we got after it. By the time the 2023 season started, we had eighty-seven new players—and fifty-seven of them came from the transfer portal.

The transfer portal to college football is what free agency is to the NFL. The world has changed. And we are keeping up with those changes. Our approach is to be as authentic and honest as possible with our young men.

We've also taken criticism over the way we use social media. But I'm sure this won't be news to you either, that social media is a way of life for this generation. We are a transparent program. We're going to showcase what we do and show people who we are. It has helped put us on the map and I haven't found too many athletes who dislike attention.

Now, are these the elements that are going to win you a national championship? No. They are simply tools to make you better, and we're going to explore every possible edge. Because OUR GOAL is just like YOUR GOAL—we all need to get a little better every day.

I think all the right things are in place at Colorado—the facilities, the school, the resources. We just need to make everybody believe in that dream.

I'm very appreciative of the opportunity given to me by Rick George, my athletic director. If you haven't noticed, there aren't a lot of Black head coaches hired to coach a college football team. And we don't exactly have a lot of wiggle room either. The Black coaches who have been fired are almost never replaced by another Black coach.

So, we're dreaming BIG.

Coach Prime as a national champion . . . at Colorado? A few years ago, nobody could've seen that one coming. Just like nobody could've imagined me coaching at Jackson State, an HBCU program. We had an amazing three seasons. To me, our success was emblematic of the words we put on our helmets:

IBELIEVE.

My goal for Jackson State was clear from Day One—we wanted to win, and win RIGHT NOW. We wanted to wake it up and capture some of its potential. But we also wanted to challenge the belief that HBCUs were some sort of inferior product. THEY ARE NOT . . . and we proved that.

I never thought too deeply about my next step because my focus was on turning Jackson State into a powerhouse. When we were on our way to winning our second straight SWAC championship, I was brutally honest when people kept asking about my future. If a tremendous opportunity came along, I'd be crazy not to consider it. And that was mostly because of opportunities for others—like bigger salaries for my coaches—instead of myself.

What was the dream? We wanted equality. We made some strides there. We wanted these kids to get notoriety and get to the NFL. The team got better, but it needs to improve even more. We were obviously underfunded and overlooked, but we improved our facilities. I want improvement for all the HBCUs, and what we accomplished at Jackson State started a conversation around the whole country. We got attention that the HBCUs had never seen before. We achieved some RELEVANCE and NOR-MALCY.

My dream was about belief. I believed we could win—and we

did. I believed we could graduate at a good rate while raising these kids to be productive young men. That's happening, too.

But to get the DREAM, you've got to DO.

So here's my lesson for you. Don't just HOPE for your dreams to come true. VISUALIZE yourself getting to your own end zone. Surround yourself with like-minded people on your team. Put your plans into action. BELIEVE. Always believe. Don't settle for average. If you do those things, I promise you, success will come your way.

COACH PRIME'S TAKEAWAYS

1. **Don't dream AVERAGE. Dream BIG.** And always use your dreams to help lift others.

2. **You've got to believe in yourself. If you don't, who will?** There will always be people telling you to stay in your lane. They're looking to shoot holes in your dream. Don't allow them to do that. Be somebody who MAKES IT HAPPEN, not one of those critics who sits on the fence and does nothing but complain.

3. **Life is really a series of moments and some of them are bigger than others. You need to identify YOUR big moments and be ready to meet them when they happen.** Prepare yourself. When your big moment happens, BE READY.

4. **I always wanted to be DIFFERENT. Don't be scared of that.** Blending in never seemed like much fun. If you're a creator or an innovator, there will always be people who laugh at you and say you're crazy. But creators and innovators are the people who change the world. Be one of those people. Be different.

5. **Sometimes, sticking to your dream requires a tremendous amount of discipline and restraint.** Sometimes, it's easy to give up, particularly if you never see any encouragement. Keep dreaming, but don't just live in some fantasy world. You need GOALS and you must WORK to make those dreams come true.

CHAPTER 18

Time Is a Wonderful Storyteller

Want to be successful? Then you better be CONSISTENT. I don't care who you are—a doctor, a lawyer, a business owner, a teacher, a parent, a professional athlete, a coach, whatever—the ability to bring your best EVERY SINGLE DAY will be the most important factor that defines your level of success.

You can't fake your way to consistency. Your consistency is best measured over time.

And trust me, time is a wonderful storyteller.

You see, most people are living double lives.

Y'all need to hear that once again.

Most people are living DOUBLE LIVES.

I'm gonna keep this 100 for y'all. I can already hear you out there. "Maybe that's true, but that ain't me!"

Well, you aren't even going to recognize what's going on until you identify with who you are, what you are, how you are, why you are, where you are, where you're going, and how to get there. Until you know all of that for sure, you're going to have a problem.

When you find out who you really are, it becomes much easier to be consistent. When you're in that search for your identity, when you're wearing a costume and doing all that TRICK-OR-TREATING, it's hard to be THIS or do THAT. You forget. Wait a minute, I was THIS to my friend, not THAT.

Darn, I'm all confused.

The Bible says, "A double-minded man is unstable in all his ways." It's hard to be stable when we practice hypocrisy and lead an insincere life. When there's no stability, there's no consistency.

You know those women who wear all that mascara, the extensions, the lashes? They're presenting something they AREN'T. And those men who seem so confident, articulate, smooth, and savvy. Oftentimes, that's NOT who they are. When everybody leaves, they're probably saying, "Thank God they're gone. Now I can just be me."

You should NEVER be that way.

I think that's what infuriates people most about me. In a hypocritical world where fake is applauded, I am always unapologetically me. I'm not trying to be anybody else. When I'm in a room with white people, Black people, Asian people, or Hispanic people, I'm still me. I ain't changing.

This is how God created me. This is what He wanted. And I'm going to give Him everything He wants. God only made one me. Through the trials and tribulations of life, I've come to enjoy myself. I've come to respect myself. And I've come to like myself.

It ain't always been this way. Earlier in my life, it was MUCH easier to be consistent on the field than it was off the field. Back then, I was trying to please two masters. I was trying to be two people simultaneously—and you can't be Deion and Prime at the same time.

Because one has an appetite for this and the other has an appetite for that. I was trying too hard to be who I THOUGHT they wanted me to be . . . instead of just being me and accepting that. No wonder I had no peace and was so unhappy.

Maybe y'all relate to that?

It's flat-out EXHAUSTING to try being something you just AIN'T. Now, being consistent isn't that easy at first either, but once you find your rhythm, once you start finding out who you really are, it's like brushing your teeth.

It might sound simple. Just do something repeatedly, over and over, get into your routine and stay there. It can be one of the toughest things to master. Every day has a different name. Every month has a different name.

And when you think about it, the challenge is being consistent in a world full of inconsistencies.

When you look in the mirror and identify who you are, you're coming to one conclusion. You AREN'T gonna be perfect. None of us are. We're ALL a work in progress.

So, the best thing you can do is be unapologetically who you are and work on your shortcomings. Me? I have no patience. I KNOW I have no patience. If I find myself in a bad situation, one that requires a lot of patience, almost like a little kid, I've learned when to take a time-out. At this age and stage of my life, I instinctively know how to make this work.

I might be your coach, but I CAN'T coach you to know exactly who you are and how to live your life. I CAN give you the license and wisdom to help accept who you are.

The one generality I can say for everybody is STOP trying to be perfect. Just quit that. There's nobody perfect out there and it's a waste of time. You don't need perfection. Your goal is consistency and being who you really are.

So how can you get consistent? I like to think of it in twenty-one-day increments. That's three weeks. Not forever, but long enough to create a routine. If I work out for twenty-one days, it's now a habit. It's the consistency of working out for twenty-one straight days or three straight weeks. I have now created something that is gonna be hard to break.

Not everything in life becomes a task, so you gotta carry it over to your daily attitude. Your actions are an interpretation of your thoughts. Therefore, you are usually showing people who you RE-ALLY ARE on a daily basis.

And I always say when somebody shows you a certain personality over time, you should BELIEVE THAT.

What you don't want to be is an adult who still enjoys a seesaw. Or one of those people who are up and down, up and down in an unpredictable way, riding that emotional roller coaster. Now look, we're all gonna have bad moments from time to time, but you don't want people walking on eggshells around you, scared of the kind of person they might be getting.

You want to be dependable, evenhanded, and somebody who reacts to things in the appropriate way. You want to handle the great moments with humility and the tough moments with grace.

Let me ask you this: If you were treated according to your consistency, would you be treated well or not?

Over time, you are who you are. Over time, it will be PROVEN who you are. It's gonna come out, sooner or later. Remember what I said: Time is a wonderful storyteller.

Own Your Strengths and Weaknesses

I don't care if you're the most famous athlete who ever lived, the leader of a multibillion-dollar business, a beloved teacher, a single mama who's trying to keep it together, or a teenager who doesn't have a clue about their future, we ALL have something in common.

We all have strengths—the skills and talents that set us apart.

And we all have weaknesses—those areas where we continually struggle, those places where we're convinced we'll never thrive.

As you live your life of consistency, don't you dare WASTE TIME trying to be someone YOU ARE NOT! I know it's tough to resist keeping up with the next man or woman, those Joneses, and presenting ourselves in the best possible light. But if it's a well-disguised lie, it just ain't worth it.

When you're doing a self-audit, you need to know what you're good at AND what you're not good at. In fact, you should be GREAT at what you know, but EVEN BETTER at realizing what you don't know.

Everybody can relate to playing to their strengths, right?

That's where you're most confident and comfortable. These are the skills that make you unique. Don't be afraid to show them off and even use them to your advantage. It's a terrible thing when you don't exercise the gift. You have some talents, but you gotta exercise them and go get it. It's on YOU! It's not on Mama. It's not on Daddy. It's not on your homies. If you got something inside of you that's just screaming to get out, it's about time YOU do something about that.

Now, what are you going to do about those weaknesses? Those are the things that might hold you back. *I'm terrible at math! I have an awful voice! I'm too short to be good at sports!* Yeah, yeah. That sounds like WHINING to me.

Don't talk yourself out of trying something just because you believe you got no shot.

Look, you've got to use your weaknesses as motivation. Use them to PUSH YOURSELF to be even better. Work on them constantly (very quietly works well, then you can SURPRISE your friends with your big improvement). You are going to get better now. I guarantee it! Don't be afraid to ask for help.

You're going to be surprised how you can ACCOMPLISH big things in areas where you thought you were terrible.

What am I even talking about?

If you're hesitant to try public speaking, take a speech class to build up your confidence. Start small, then make it into a strength to give presentations at work or volunteer to speak at community events. Show up CONSISTENTLY and you'll get SO MUCH better.

If you're not good at math, find a tutor or take a class to improve your skills. Have it explained at your pace, and as a result, you'll probably find that you can get the hang of it.

Work on it CONSISTENTLY.

If you're shy, join a club or take a class where you can meet new people and practice socializing. Be CONSISTENT in attending those meetings.

If you're out of shape, start walking—even if it's back and forth to your mailbox. Add to your pace each day. Be CONSISTENT with it. It won't be long until you're walking a few miles and maybe even jogging.

The important thing is not letting your weaknesses hold you back and keep you from becoming all you were meant to be. And don't let your strengths go unused. We were all given gifts and we need to take advantage of them.

Take Responsibility for Yourself

We all make excuses. It's just human nature. When we have a plan and then something changes, we're all quick to point out how life isn't fair, how the world is against us, how it's not our fault, all that nonsense.

It drives me crazy.

You know what's the WORST?

When somebody becomes one of those "I'd a . . ." people.

What's that mean?

If I hadn't smoked all that weed, I'd a been this.

If that teacher wasn't against me, I'd a been that.

If I hadn't been drinking so darn much, I'd a been this.

If my boss hadn't given the job to his buddy, I'd a been that.

There's only one person who's in charge of your life.

You.

If you want consistency in your life, you gotta TAKE RESPON-SIBILITY for yourself—period. There ain't no asterisks or excuses next to this one. It's all about YOU—for better or worse, as they say.

To this day, I'm still haunted a bit by what happened to the Prime Prep Academy, a group of charter schools in the Dallas area that I cofounded back in 2012. Our goal was to help a bunch of kids by giving them the foundation for a successful life through academics and athletics.

Due to a lack of oversight, we had to close it in 2015. And that was on me. My name was on that building, and I should've been watching things more carefully. I thought we had the right people to handle the business part and finances. But we DIDN'T.

While it was a painful and humbling lesson, looking back I can now say that it was the best thing to ever happen to me, because of the kids we were able to help. We learned from our mistakes, and I feel it made us all a lot better.

It's disheartening to put your stamp on something like that and see it fall apart, but it showed me that you must be accountable for your actions. You've got to own it. Even your failures. Especially your failures.

So, what do you do when your dreams and goals fall short? Where can you turn when your plans go sideways?

Here are a few ways you can get better:

- **Be honest with yourself**—This is number one. You may be in denial that it ain't your fault and you're the victim of some elaborate conspiracy, but sooner or later, you're going to realize the truth. DON'T make excuses and DON'T blame other people for your problems. Own it! Be honest with yourself. Take a close look at your own behavior and pick out the areas where you need to improve. Then DO SOME-THING ABOUT IT.

- **Be accountable**—Once you look at those areas where you want to improve, make your plan to address them. Then HOLD YOURSELF ACCOUNTABLE by following through on your plan.

- **Learn from your mistakes**—When things go wrong—and they will—don't view it as a disaster. Make it into a LEARNING EXPERIENCE. Failure is NOT fatal. It's very often the first step toward success. So, treat it in that manner and never give up or just walk away.

- **Take action**—Don't just sit around and wait for something to happen. Stop standing still. Take steps every day to get closer to your goals.

- **Celebrate your success**—Even if it's a small thing, give yourself a REWARD. If you're going to take responsibility when things go wrong, then you deserve to celebrate when things go right.

If you show the CONSISTENCY of taking responsibility for yourself, you're showing me one of my favorite qualities for any person.

Character.

I like work ethic. I certainly like to hire talent. But I LOVE character.

You want to stand out? If you possess great character, you will be a person who is UNSTOPPABLE. You won't be distracted by any external forces because you'll listen to your heart. That will allow you to wipe away your tears during the difficult moments and know that NOBODY can stop you, even when it seems like the world is full of naysayers.

Being mature. Taking responsibility for yourself. The consistency of character. You just CAN'T BEAT those special qualities.

Keep Your Promises

How often does THIS happen to you? Somebody makes you a promise. Maybe they commit to a deadline on a project at work. They say don't worry about anything. They got your back.

Then they don't.

When you call them on it, they look at you like you're crazy and say they have no memory of making that promise.

Well, how about that? Were you just IMAGINING that promise? Nope.

Being consistent means you're a person of integrity. It means you're dependable. It means you're a person of your word—and you'll never, ever go back on it.

When you promise something to somebody, when you speak it into existence, you have an OBLIGATION to keep that promise. You don't back away from that. You make good on it. And if something goes wrong, then you need to figure out a way to make it right.

Keeping your promises shows that you are a person of character. It shows that you are reliable and trustworthy.

You're automatically going to be more POPULAR because who doesn't want to be around someone they know they can count on—no matter what?

Keeping your promises also leads to trust. When people know they can trust you, it always leads to better opportunities and relationships.

And, of course, keeping your promises will make you feel good about yourself. When you do what you say you're going to do, it gives you a sense of accomplishment and satisfaction.

So how can you make SURE you maintain your character and integrity, that you're viewed as that wonderful person who always keeps their promises?

Think before making a promise—Don't make a promise unless you're sure you can keep it. Your words carry weight, so don't overcommit yourself. Be realistic.

Plan ahead—If you know you have a lot of commitments coming up, take some time to plan your schedule to make sure you can keep all your promises. Don't wait until it's too late and things start piling up.

Be flexible—Sometimes, things don't go according to plan. It might be out of your control. So be prepared to adjust your schedule or commitments as needed.

Communicate—Let the person know—as early as possible—if you're going to be late or you can't keep the promise for some reason. Be sure to apologize if the fates work against you, then find some way to make it right.

Ask for help—Don't be too proud to take on everything yourself. If you're feeling overwhelmed, ask for help from friends, family, or colleagues.

Promise me y'all are going to do these things, OK? Because that will set you up as a person who keeps their promises. And that means a lot.

COACH PRIME'S TAKEAWAYS

1. **You can't fake your way to CONSISTENCY.** Leading a consistent life will show itself over time. And time is a wonderful storyteller.

2. **Believe it or not, most people lead double lives.** And that's where the major problems come in. Look, it's exhausting to be something you AREN'T. So, you've got to figure out who you are—and be that person EVERY SINGLE DAY. Stop trying to be so perfect. There are no perfect people out there. Just be yourself. That's enough.

3. **We all have strengths and weaknesses. The trick is exploiting those strengths and showing them off.** That's what makes you unique. Learn from those weaknesses and don't be afraid to fail. You should be GREAT at what you know, but EVEN BETTER at realizing what you don't know.

4. **One person should take responsibility for your life—and that's YOU.** Don't blame others. Don't play the victim. Be responsible for your own success and hold yourself accountable for living up to your standard.

5. **Keeping your promises is the best way to show you are a consistent person of INTEGRITY.** Be sure not to overcommit yourself and always try to keep things realistic. But if you make a promise to someone, it's on you to live up to that trust, even if it means some extra communication and flexibility to make it happen in these busy times for everyone.

CHAPTER 19

Thriving in a Diverse World

One thing I've learned in coaching and in life: Everyone moves to their own beat. To get the most from those around you, it's important to understand their beat.

As a society, we AREN'T meant to all be the same. Diversity has become a huge thing in schools and in the workplace, and I'm a true believer that all those varying viewpoints make things better. On this subject, athletics has often led the way. I've always said if you want to learn how to get along with all sorts of people, if you want to bring different backgrounds together for a common goal, you should play sports. Diversity is what makes us stronger.

You gotta remember, I'M OLD SCHOOL, not an OLD FOOL. I know that times have shifted. I'm not changing my approach, but I know the way I communicate must be different at times. If you don't know how somebody ticks, you can't get the most out of them. One size DOES NOT fit all.

These days, you've got to meet people where they are. If you're a teacher or a boss, I'm not telling you anything new here. Sometimes you've got to go around the corner with people. Back in the day, we just went straight there. Today's young people are a little different. You can't put them all in a group and address them the same way.

It's true in the workplace, too. Some people respond well to the direct approach. Others are thinkers. They're calculating. It's like they're playing chess and you've got to stay one move ahead of them. Instead of treating it as one big group, it's really like a dozen different relationships.

You've seen it, right?

Some people can be told something one time and they just want to be left alone to complete the task. Others have a million questions, and they need to constantly check to make sure it's going well. Then you've got people who get a little distracted and unfocused. Those are the ones you've got to check back with and make sure they're on track.

It's not like the old-time teachers who ruled their classroom and could send any bad-behavior kids away for a good paddling. It's not like the old-time coaches who were all-powerful and never got questioned. And I'm sure it's not like the old-time bosses who motivated through fear and reigned over a roomful of people who needed to pay their mortgage and feed their family.

Now everybody wants to question things. They want to know . . . "Why? Why are we doing this? Why are we doing that?" As a leader, it can sometimes drive you crazy. Dealing with different personalities can be a real challenge.

You've got your extroverts, who are outgoing, talkative, and social. You've got your introverts, who get their energy from being alone and having time to be thoughtful. Some folks are practical and detail-oriented. Some folks are creative, imaginative, and big-picture thinkers. Some folks are logical and analytical. Some folks are built around emotions, relationships, empathy, and compassion.

That's a FULL room.

You've got to know who wants to lead, who wants to be social, who needs to be left alone, who wants to be creative and autonomous, and who wants clear rules and expectations. Which approach is correct? The answer is . . . there is no right answer. But there is a right way to juggle different personalities.

First and foremost, be respectful of everyone's differences. Don't try to change them. Be patient with everyone. It takes time to build relationships and learn what's best for everyone. We all have unique strengths and weaknesses. That's how our world rolls. Everyone has their own tick.

The Other Side of the Story

It's so easy to judge people based on what we see on the surface. We see someone who is successful, and we automatically think they have it all together. At the same time, we see someone who is struggling, and we think they're a failure.

The truth is we don't know what's going on behind closed doors. We don't know what someone is going through. We DON'T know their whole story.

So, before we judge someone, we need to take a step back and try to understand their situation. We need to see things from their perspective.

Remember that everyone is fighting some kind of battle. Everyone is dealing with something. If you see somebody at your workplace with their head down on their desk, it's easy to think they have a hangover or they stayed out too late the night before. But maybe they just received terrible news and they're not sure how to deal with it.

So never assume anything—no matter how it looks.

Just because someone is successful, they still can be dealing with more problems than a math book. Let me say that again. Just because someone SEEMS successful, they can still be dealing WITH MORE PROBLEMS than a math book. And just because someone is struggling, it doesn't automatically mean they're a failure.

The thing that really shocks us is how public success sometimes hides private struggles. We see people on TV or on social media and they seem to have everything they could ever want. But the truth is many successful people are dealing with addiction, depression, anxiety, and other mental health issues. They might be struggling with relationships, finances, or even their careers. The next time you see someone who looks like they have it all, just remember that they might be struggling behind closed doors.

Instead of being quick to judge, let's not point fingers. Let's just be there for each other. Always try to see things from someone else's perspective. The way you can really help is by being kind, supportive, and understanding.

Judging others is not only unfair, but it can also be harmful. When we judge others, we're basically saying that we're better than them. We're putting them down and making them feel bad about themselves.

So, hold back those judgments. Bring some understanding. In a small way that's very big for other people, we're making the world a better place.

Be Willing to Change

In an ever-changing world, there's a HUGE benefit to knowing how someone ticks. If you can intuitively make that connection, then you'll always know how to find the best approach for any situation. That's about as valuable a skill as you could have.

There's only one thing constant in our lives—and that is CHANGE. It's happening all around us, all the time. And it's not just happening in the workplace. It's happening in our personal lives, too.

We ALL say we're willing to change.

We ALL say we want change.

Then change comes along and it makes us uncomfortable. Then we're singing a different tune.

Think about how different life was just thirty years ago. The Internet was just getting started, and there was no social media, no cell phone in everybody's pocket (it wouldn't have fit). Just think how much our daily lives have changed in that time.

Think about how different life was before the pandemic. Shopping changed forever. Are your neighborhood streets clogged with delivery trucks? Are you getting groceries and your dinner dropped at your door? How much do you work at home and communicate on Zoom instead of going into the office? Do you ever go hang out at the mall anymore? Man, they're even talking about malls going away one day. Blows my mind!

What's next? What's this artificial intelligence thing gonna mean? Is broadcast TV going away completely and will we be streaming EVERYTHING on a computer? How much longer will we be carrying dollar bills and coins before they make us pay for everything by tapping our phones?

HOW DO WE ADAPT to all this change? How do we make sure we don't get left behind and we don't get perceived as that get-off-my-lawn person?

- **First, we need to be OPEN to change**—We should be willing to embrace new things and new ideas and not fear it.

- **Second, we need to be FLEXIBLE**—Let's adapt our thinking and our behavior to meet the changing circumstances—and not stress about it.

- **Third, we need to be resilient**—You get stronger by bouncing back from setbacks and disappointments.

These are all important qualities because change IS NOT easy. It can be disruptive and uncomfortable. But you know what? It's also an opportunity for growth and development.

When we adapt to change, we become stronger and more capable. Once we do it, it doesn't seem nearly as bad as we had imagined. So that gives us more CONFIDENCE to handle any crazy thing life throws our way.

This is important, y'all: DON'T be afraid of change. Embrace it. Welcome it. At least have an open mind. You might be surprised at how it works out.

Now let's swing this over to the workplace. As you know, workplaces are CONSTANTLY changing. Technology is exploding. The way we do business is sometimes unrecognizable. The expectations of our customers and clients are changing. So what the heck are we going to do?

It's time to EVOLVE, y'all. What's that you're saying? "Oh, I can't change. I'm scared of doing it differently."

Just look at how I've changed. I was a kid from the inner city, just clinging to a dream. I put myself out there as "Prime Time"—after being given that nickname on the basketball court—and couldn't sneak up on anybody. My reputation was well known. I had it all—power, money, sex—or so I thought. In my mind, I really had nothing. I viewed myself as a failure and my life was hanging by a thread. Then I found meaning through God, through helping other people. When I was just looking to help my own kids, I found out that was my life's calling—coaching and working with ALL kids.

Now I'm in a place I couldn't have predicted and never thought I'd be—I'm a major college football coach. I'm a proud dad. I'm living my purpose. And in a way, I feel like I'm just getting started.

Change is a beautiful thing. It keeps you on your toes. It makes you into your best self. It challenges you every day.

So, here's what I'll tell y'all about change:

First and foremost, we need to stay up-to-date on the latest trends and technologies. This is a MUST. We need to be aware of the changes that are happening in our industry and in the world around us. For me, the last few years, that means Name, Image and Likeness (NIL) and the transfer portal. Those things have revolutionized college sports everywhere. If you don't adapt to them, you are not going to have any success.

Be willing to learn new things. This means being open to new ideas and new ways of doing things. The world is getting a lot smaller. We're ALL behind the times if we're not learning a second language—and I'll blame myself for this as well. No excuse.

We need to be flexible and adaptable. Those were always great qualities, but they have become even more important. There are times when you've got to tweak your thinking and behavior to meet the changing needs of business and other areas of life.

We all tend to do what we do. We're not straying far from our comfort zone, right? That's a mistake. We ALL should network with people who are different. It helps you to get fresh perspectives and learn new things.

Sometimes you've got to take risks. If you don't step out, you're always going to be standing still. Never be afraid to learn and grow.

And the thing you always need—not only for change but any part of life—is a positive attitude. That will keep you motivated and help you to overcome challenges.

The Next Generation

If you're in charge of anything these days—a football team, a business, a school—one of your biggest challenges will be dealing with the work habits, ambitions, and ideas of the next generation. It hits different. And that's probably understandable.

Back in the day, young people didn't have much of a say in anything. It was all "Do as you're told, don't question, work hard, earn your stripes." You didn't challenge adults, and if you chose to talk back, you usually paid for it.

Our kids have essentially grown up online and with those values. Not only do they have a voice, it's also often amplified. There's more entitlement than we've ever seen and more of a feeling that they know exactly what they're doing—even if they have ZERO experience.

So, what are we going to do with this, bosses?

The VERY FIRST THING—and it's the theme of this chapter—is embrace the change. Because guess what? As much as we tend to complain about the younger generation, with their supposed shaky work ethic and all the qualities we can't stand, there are some good things coming along that you probably don't hear enough about. These kids stand up for themselves. They're smart. They want inclusion, empowerment, and versatility. They're bringing more innovation instead of repeating the same old way. It's no longer about settling in for a lifetime with one company. Some of these kids change jobs the way we used to change socks. Because that's how it is in this current moment.

Like anything, dealing with the change is all about the approach. You've got to communicate. You need to be specific. Some of these folks have been rewarded for participation and effort—you've heard of participation trophies, right?—and we need to fine-tune it to make sure EVERYONE knows that we're about RESULTS. Nothing wrong or unfair about wanting results. We're a results-driven society.

But I'll also say this about our kids: This generation might be the most adaptable to change that we've ever seen. And that's a good thing. Because things are changing by the second, and if you know how to adapt, you know how to survive.

All these things should be understood by the folks who aren't in leadership roles. If you think dealing with change is difficult for a manager, just picture yourself as a rookie worker who hasn't yet proven themselves.

That might seem nerve-racking, but we're really living in the land of opportunity. You can make a career for yourself and get up to speed quickly. And if you're a technology expert—somebody who can use modern tools to make things easier around the office—you're practically invaluable.

Many of us are in a position that our parents never were. We're lucky to be further ahead. The trials and tribulations, the work ethic that was instilled in us, provoke us to give our children the things we never had. That's a blessing—and a curse.

Even with all the modern-day advantages, I find myself sometimes wishing that my kids had an inkling of the upbringing I had.

What I've tried to do with my kids is take them to the other side of town, put them in athletics, put them in different schools, trying to give them a little understanding of how Daddy came up back in the day, of how Daddy rose out of his surroundings.

Even though they still have on name-brand clothes, they need to learn these things. You're gonna need both sides to make it in life. The privileges are nice. But it's also good to know what it's like in the hood.

When I brought my son Shedeur to Jackson State, he had already lived through my inner-city youth organizations, the inner-city schools, even though we were living over here in a different place behind a gate. I'm thankful for that because my kids saw a little bit of what it was like for me.

It also made them knowledgeable about the different ways of life. When I was a kid and got an opportunity to play sports with kids from families with a much better financial background, I was really careful to stay focused, to represent my family well, and not pay attention to anything negative that might be said. I was locked in because I had come from across town to participate. I was being exposed to a part of life I had never seen before, and it helped to round me out.

I encourage y'all to expose your kids to all sorts of things in your neighborhood and far away, too. Your kids are going to see everything and renounce what they don't like. You're going to teach them some different tendencies and that will help them get along in this big, diverse world.

We've got a racial divide, an economic divide, certainly a political divide, and probably a social divide. This is the world our kids are going to inherit. But you know what? I have TONS of confidence in our young folks.

My biggest fans are the youth. I have a real affinity for bringing along young people, exposing them to different viewpoints and getting them ready for the real world. I dream about the ones who are going to get out there and create change. Y'all should feel the same way. I don't even have the vocabulary to explain how much I love it when one of my kids does something outside the box and unexpected. The world is full of different people and different approaches. The ones who succeed are the ones who can adapt and thrive in that environment.

COACH PRIME'S TAKEAWAYS

1. **We were NEVER meant to all be the same. Diversity is a huge part of our world.** Dealing with different personalities is a big part of all workplaces these days. Whether it's introverts, extroverts, or anybody in between, you've got to realize how everyone beats their own drum, then learn the best way to reach them.

2. **Judging people on the surface is never a good idea.** Most people are fighting battles we don't know about. Public success can sometimes be hiding private struggles. So DON'T ASSUME anything until you know the whole story.

3. **Change is the only constant in all our lives.** Don't hesitate to be open to change, particularly in the workplace, with the ever-evolving technology and protocol. When you ROLL WITH THE CHANGES and learn new skills, your confidence will get a boost and you'll find yourself better equipped to take on new challenges.

4. **Make it a point to network with people who are DIFFERENT.** You'll learn new perspectives, while becoming more flexible and adaptable.

5. **It's easy to stay in our own little world. Parents, prepare your kids and then push them to get out there.** That means playing and learning with kids who don't look like them. That means venturing far from your neighborhood. The future belongs to the people who can adapt to all sorts of cultures and personalities.

CHAPTER 20

Finish!

At the end of the 2022 season, after winning the SWAC championship, I gathered my Jackson State University football team into a meeting room and delivered the news that I wanted them to hear straight from the horse.

I was leaving.

Of course, it was extremely emotional. We had gone through so much together. But this happens all the time in college football. The head coach gets another job, usually with a substantial raise, and he generally leaves fast enough to form a vapor trail.

THAT'S NOT MY STYLE.

I stayed with my Jackson State team a few more weeks, until we played in the Celebration Bowl, our reward for a fantastic unbeaten season. Now, that created a bit of a hardship because I was coaching two teams at once. When I had some Zooms with Colorado, I had to make sure I had on my Colorado hat. Then I'd change into my Jackson State gear and head to practice.

Would my life have been so much easier by just getting out to Colorado, doing the recruiting and the other duties, instead of doing what everyone else does? No question.

But I had to FINISH what I started.

Although God promoted me, we still had a task at hand to complete. I felt so passionate about those young men, that program, the personnel associated with it, the fans, the alumni, and the staff. These were the young men and women who had made it possible for me to soar. It wouldn't have felt right any other way. Let's get this straight. I didn't come to Jackson to leave. I came to Jackson to win. On the path of winning, options arose and I had to weigh them.

But we had to FINISH.

Finish . . . I really love that word!

It's what I'm all about. For success and consistency in everything you do, finishing should be what YOU are all about, too.

Finishing is what we always preach—and you've got to practice what you preach.

To me, there's nothing more annoying than a task left undone. It suggests a lack of discipline, almost a lack of caring, and most definitely a lack of organization.

Have you ever started cleaning your closet, then you got bored or distracted, maybe started playing video games amid the work, then never finished? Or you're doing a project at work, you start to lose focus, then the time just gets away from you? It's frustrating because there's nothing more invigorating than finishing strong. And there's nothing more disgusting than NOT finishing because that probably means you quit. Not acceptable.

Finishing is a state of mind. It has always ignited me and motivated me.

When I used to drive back home from college, I would sometimes get a few speeding tickets. Man, I hated getting nailed, but after thinking about it, I realized I always got a ticket when I got close to my destination. There was excitement about finishing the journey. My speed increased as I got near the end!

I ran a little track in my day. After my races, they always told me my finish was so much better than my start. In football, it seemed like I got better as the game grew. You're bumping and running a guy all day long and he just wears out, but you're in shape and strong in that fourth quarter. Baseball is a very analytical game, full of statistics. The coaches always told me my sixth through ninth innings were so much better—when the game was on the line—than my first through fifth innings.

I always liked the tasks where I could see the finish line. Sometimes, coaches would just run you blindly to enforce discipline, and there was no clear end in sight. I much preferred it when they said to run five gassers. Cool. I know what that's about and I can see the prize at the end. I can get that one measured up.

We all want to be known as STRONG FINISHERS, not quitters or people who just run out of gas because we're not up to it. Finishing is the quality you want to be known for in all walks of life.

If you have the audacity to start something, you need to finish.

Winners Never Quit

One of the reasons I LOVE finishing so much is because I HATE the notion of quitting. You should feel the same way. Trust me, the one thing you DON'T want on your résumé is being a quitter.

Truth: if you quit something once, you're going to quit again. Guaranteed. When life gets tough, those same buttons will be pushed again. Because now the devil has your address.

There are so many times in life when you're working hard and nothing is happening. There are no results. It seems like you're running in place. So, the natural tendency is to want to quit and cut your losses.

Don't do it!

I've been in that situation. Working my butt off. Nothing going right. But you know what? I never gave up. I kept pushing forward and I eventually saw some results.

If you give up, you'll always wonder what might have been.

You'll never know how far you could've gone. If you're the boss at work or if you're a parent, it's up to you to set the example. The younger people who look up to you are going to follow your lead. If you quit, so will they.

So when the going gets tough, how can you stay inspired to keep on trying when your mind and body are begging to surrender?

- **Establish realistic goals** — If you're too ambitious or unrealistic, you might set yourself up for failure. Don't try to reinvent the wheel or create a world record for production in one day. By achieving small goals, you'll gain the confidence to gradually work up to larger goals. And when you break up those goals into smaller steps, it's going to seem a lot less daunting.

- **Be sure to track your progress** — Obviously, when your goal is finishing, anything short of that won't seem very impressive. But if you see some progress, even small progress, that will help you stay positive and motivated.

- **Don't compare yourself to others** — Everyone's journey is different. Focus on your own progress and don't worry about what others are doing. As they say, where you start often isn't where you finish. Some students make remarkable improvement from their freshman to senior years. Some workers might seem like a disaster when they first start, but once they learn the ropes and company culture, they can transform themselves into invaluable assets.

Just imagine what would have been missed if they had quit.

There once was a cartoonist who faced many failures. His first company went bankrupt. He went years without selling any work or getting much traction at all. Finally, he created a character called Mickey Mouse . . . and that cartoonist found his niche.

Good thing WALT DISNEY kept at it.

There once was a singer who was so excited when she produced her first album. Unfortunately, that album only sold two hundred copies before the record label went out of business. Then she was dropped from two other labels. It took nearly ten years before she recorded her first hit song.

KATY PERRY kept performing when she easily could've tried something else.

There once was an actor who had a tough time early in his career. He was homeless for three weeks, living in a bus station. While he was laboring over a script, his electricity was turned off. SYLVESTER STALLONE never gave up. The script, by the way, was *Rocky*.

There are so many inspirational examples I could list here. These are just a few that come to mind. Remember this: Life is never going to be easy. There will be pain either way, whether it's the pain of discipline or the pain of regret.

Choose discipline and persistence.

Don't quit.

Everything in Life Moves Forward

When you move, good things usually happen.

When you hesitate, that usually means trouble.

To finish ANYTHING requires movement, action, and decisiveness. Too many people just sit in their chairs, being mesmerized by their television or their phone, just watching their life melt away and not doing anything in the name of progress.

So . . . MOVE!

What's your level of speed? In football terms, you need to be running before you even get to the field, and moving between drills. Everything else needs to go-go-go at a great pace.

If you're standing still, you're actually going backwards because our world is moving at a fast pace.

Zig Ziglar, the great motivational writer and speaker, once said, "I move forward in my life every day, even if it's only a tiny step, because I know that great things are accomplished with tiny moves, but nothing is accomplished by standing still."

Let that one sink in.

NOTHING IS ACCOMPLISHED BY STANDING STILL.

Everything points forward. The days go from Sunday to Monday to Tuesday. The calendar runs from January through December. The clock doesn't run backward. You know that sound when a truck is backing up? *Beep-beep-beep.* It's like a warning. I'M GOING THE WRONG WAY! We're supposed to be progressive. When we're idle, that's when we notice a problem. The capacity for advancement is what life is all about.

For me, these things are God-ordained. God whispers to me about certain things, and I can hear clearly about the whole concept of positive movement.

I felt that kind of energy before my first NFL game with the Atlanta Falcons. It was a special occasion, so I got me one of those Rolex watches. Iced-out diamonds everywhere. It was nice!

But when I went to put it on with an outfit that matched, it didn't work.

I called the jeweler in a rage. I was livid! I couldn't believe I got ripped off like that. Then he said, "Prime, calm down. Move your wrist. OK, now move it again." Once I moved my wrist, the watch started to function. I saw the hands start ticking as the watch was movement-activated. Once I understood this, I apologized for tearing into him. I said, "Okay, I appreciate you" in embarrassment. I didn't understand that the Rolex was based on movement.

What I knew from that moment on is that when you MOVE, things work. Spiritually, I don't allow the enemy to get a good shot at me. I'm not a hunter. I don't kill or do anything like that. But I do know it's easier to hit a stationary target instead of a moving target.

And so I keep moving. I keep advancing. I keep going. I keep sidestepping haters and naysayers. I keep dodging bullets that were meant to destroy me.

Look, plenty of people choose to be still because they think that's safe. You're NEVER going to stub your toe while you're standing still. The faster you go, of course, the greater chance you have of getting hurt. But the only way to get somewhere meaningful is to move forward.

That's why you shouldn't dwell on any one thing. Sometimes, you've had the best day ever at work or with your family. Sometimes, you just want to put your head down on the desk, or not get outta bed cause you're having problems with the kids. Either way, these are very temporary things. It doesn't matter which one happened, you just move ahead to the next activity. It's the same thing in sports. You never want to be gloating over a victory or sulking over a loss. That's the equivalent of standing still.

I can only think of one occasion where time stands still—and that's eternity. That's the place we're all trying to go. But here on earth, make it a habit to keep moving forward. That's how you get ahead.

Enjoy the Process

My greatest fear? Not finishing something. Having a very important task go undone. I've got to put a period—or preferably, an exclamation mark—at the end of everything I've started.

I want to complete my mission here on earth, touching and influencing as many lives as I possibly can. I'm not sure if I'll ever really know the true definition of "retirement." Are you retired from what you once did? Are you just tired? What if you still have a lot to give? I'm not sure if I could adapt to that lifestyle when I knew there was more left in my tank.

Here's where I think we need to get our minds right. It's very invigorating to finish a task in the right way and know you brought it to a great conclusion. There's satisfaction in knowing you didn't quit, and you can read your results on the scoreboard.

But we've also got to enjoy the process. Or else what's the point of this thing we call life?

As you likely know, GPS is a navigational system where you can plot out your journey. You punch in an address, and it spits out the route. It tells us where to turn and what we're going to encounter. It tells us where the gas stations and restaurants are located. It even computes our arrival time. You're making a long trip to see somebody, and you let them know, "It says I'm going to be on your doorstep at four thirty, so I'll see you then."

Once upon a time, we used to all drive around with a map under the floor mat or in the glove compartment that helped us get where we needed to go. It was tough to see the end from the beginning. Sometimes it was confusing. You'd either go the wrong way or you might have to stop at a gas station and ask for directions. Then you'd go to a phone booth—that's a story for another time, all you young folks—and say you got lost and were running late.

There's no question that today's navigational system has made our lives more efficient. We are driven to get to the finish and we know what's ahead, right down to the minute. It reminds me of a lot of other things in our lives where we can see the finish line, such as the academic world, where you're always advancing through the grades with a goal of getting through high school and on to college so you can determine your path in life.

That's all well and good. But we need to make sure the end

point isn't our only goal. The journey itself is where we learn all the lessons of life. The ups and downs, the bumps and bruises, that's where we develop our character, our experiences, and our memories.

It's important to set goals, but it's equally important to be present in the process toward achieving those goals. Part of that process is making mistakes, and that's where you learn the most. There's something to be gained from all your experiences—good and bad.

When you get to the end of your career or journey, when you earn the prize and you're reflecting on what it took to finally reach that finish line, it's always about the people you met along the way and the experiences that helped shape you. Those are the important parts of our development as human beings.

Part of the satisfaction of finishing is looking back at how we overcame the obstacles and how we prevailed.

The other point I want to leave you with is that sometimes it's not in your best interest to finish. Now, I know you're thinking, *Coach Prime, what are you even talking about? You got me to the point where I'm all about finishing everything I start and now you're saying there are times when I should just give it up?*

Let me explain.

There are times in life when we shouldn't have started something in the first place. It usually has something to do with relationships.

This can be a volatile subject, but a lot of people stay in relationships longer than they need to. The quality of finishing is inside them, so they don't give up. But some situations present themselves as toxic and ignorant and you've got to get out. Obviously, if someone is trying to bring harm to you or your children, that's the signal right there.

This is when you need to understand the difference between finishing and being smart. This is when you need to realize you shouldn't have started this thing in the first place. So, on those occasions, I don't think you should be held accountable for not finishing.

What is finishing as a parent? You know, I've seen some great parents who raised their kids so well, and because of circumstances like divorce they weren't even in the home all the time. But they were still great parents.

The basic instinct is always to finish the task. But there are times when you need to pray for guidance and wisdom to know whether it's best to finish at all costs or go in a different direction.

COACH PRIME'S TAKEAWAYS

1. **Always finish what you start in life.** You want to put that period—or maybe that exclamation point—at the end of every sentence. FINISHING will give you success and consistency in everything you do.

2. **If you quit something once, the odds are great that you'll quit again. So . . . DON'T QUIT.** No matter how difficult the task seems, stay on point because the finish line might be closer than it seems.

3. **Everything in life moves FORWARD.** So don't hesitate or become idle. Keep moving. Keep advancing. That's how you make progress.

4. **Finishing is always the end goal. But remember to enjoy the PROCESS and the JOURNEY.** There's a lot to be learned along the way and be careful not to miss all those lessons.

5. **Sometimes you do have to abort the mission.** It might be a toxic relationship or a situation that's going to have bad results. This is where you need to pray for the WISDOM TO KNOW whether it's best to finish at all costs or go in a different direction.

CHAPTER 21

Find Your Peace

Faith brings you peace. I've always had faith—at least I thought I did.

When I was a kid, it was Friendship Baptist Church in Fort Myers. I remember walking down the street with my sister, Tracie, who would get us both to church every Sunday if our mama wasn't available. Everybody in the neighborhood was there. Attendance was mandatory.

I didn't really understand who Christ was, but I always had a reverence for the Lord. Even in college, I always read one Bible verse daily. That was just my way of staying connected to Christ and feeling good about myself.

It really wasn't authentic because I didn't truly have a relationship with the Lord. The stuff I did was like a Band-Aid or anesthetic for the pain I was feeling or the things I would do. I might have been READING those verses, but I sure wasn't LIVING those verses.

You know, it was like, "I'm going to read some scripture and that will make me feel better for the life I am living." If you asked me five minutes later what verse I read, I couldn't recall it. I still thought I had a reverence for the Lord. But for me, this was just a practice, a repetition, not a LIFESTYLE.

I *believed* I was a believer. I truly did. But I wasn't ready to commit. Because COMMITTING means SUBMITTING. Even if I was ready to commit, I wasn't ready to submit and give up some of the things that brought me pleasure.

At that point in my life, I hadn't seen the Christians who enjoyed their lives. It was always like, "If you're a Christian, you can't do this!" There was always a rule book. It seemed like you were in jail. This wasn't the way to follow the God I thought I knew. It just wasn't fun at all, and I completely didn't see it.

If I were to be completely honest, I didn't have faith OR peace in my life at that time. To find those qualities, I had to go as low as you could possibly go. I had it all, right? I was a well-paid professional athlete, a cultural icon, surrounded by all the opulence you could ever imagine, women everywhere, living in the finest homes, driving the best-looking cars, knowing that I had financial security for myself and my family.

But I was beyond miserable. I spent years with fake smiles and false bravado. It took me a long, long time to even realize that I needed help because it was hard to imagine. Didn't I have the life I'd always dreamed of? Wasn't I rich and famous? The more I acquired, the more unhappy I became. So, I tried to push away my unhappiness and that only made it worse.

It was like a leaky faucet that went drip-drip-drip. What's a few drips? But if you let it go for years and years, you got a flood on your hands.

In 1997, when I believed that all the love had been taken out of my life—my first marriage was dissolving and my wife was threatening to take away our two children—when I was convinced that NOBODY cared whether I lived or died, I thought there was only one decision remaining.

I drove my beautiful custom-made black Mercedes off a cliff. Suicide was never something I had imagined. But in that moment, I didn't see a way out.

I wanted it to be the end. But through the grace of God, it was the beginning.

The beginning of something GLORIOUS.

A Plunge . . . Then an Ascension

Up until that point, my longtime agent, Eugene Parker, who was one of the sincerest Christian people I had ever encountered, had known that faith was the answer for me. But I wasn't buying into that. I just wasn't.

God kept calling collect and I refused to answer. I didn't want to. I had never been a phony and I wasn't about to start faking it. I wasn't ready to give up some of the things I was doing. Some people of faith had misrepresented themselves to be perfect, without sin, without blemish. That's the way I thought you had to be. That's what kept me from coming all the way home.

I felt my life was in complete crisis. My wife, Carolyn, wanted a divorce. I was upset that the only two people who I felt REALLY loved me—my kids—were going to be taken away.

I was in Cincinnati, playing baseball for the Reds. But I wasn't thinking about baseball. I wasn't thinking about anything but my kids and how I was about to lose the only thing in my life that really mattered.

Mentally, I was running out of gas. I was leaking oil. I felt completely isolated. I was a high-profile professional athlete. I could go out and come home with a woman, but I always knew those women just loved the lifestyle and the money. They didn't love me. The fans cheered for the player, but they never knew the person. And they really didn't love me either.

My kids loved me because I was Daddy. They were the one thing in my life that truly had my back. Now I'm looking at my wife taking them away from me and moving to another city. I couldn't even conceive of how a court would allow it, letting the mother do her own thing and splitting up the family.

That's what I was feeling on this particular dark night.

And that's when I started to think, *You know what? I wonder if anybody would care if I wasn't here? These people just care about how I perform. They don't care about me as a person.*

That's when the enemy began applying pressure with the suicidal thoughts. He just needs the seed to be planted and then he applies the pressure.

I think everybody has those thoughts from time to time. *What if I wasn't even here? Would anyone even care?* But those are usually just passing thoughts. Most people don't act on them.

Here's what I truly believe: The enemy had to bring this level of attack to try and kill me because he KNEW what would happen if I lived. I was going to have influence and help a lot of people come to the Lord. He DID NOT want this new chapter of my life to start.

If I got over this hump, I was going to sell out for the Lord with a whole new family and some peace in my life. I was going to have a tremendous positive impact on a multitude of people. So that's why the enemy upped the ante.

He almost won. I was a mess, an absolute mess. I wasn't strong when I really needed to be strong. I gave in to the pain.

My mind was racing. None of the stuff I had been chasing meant anything to me. I felt like such a failure.

I decided I'd had enough. I was running on fumes and had pretty much lost all hope.

What was my game plan? I jumped in my Mercedes, got on the open road, and floored it. I was doing about sixty-five or seventy, and that's when it came to me.

I was going to end this quickly. I would drive off a cliff, everything would go black, and my pain would finally go away.

When I went over the cliff, I was playing Kirk Franklin's urban gospel song "Conquerors."

Man, talk about a contradiction at its finest!

Well, my game plan FAILED MISERABLY. And that was all God. It HAD to be all God. The drop was thirty or forty feet. Somehow I survived and there wasn't a scratch on me. There's no question about it, even for a nonbeliever: God had His hands on me.

You drive at a fast speed, you veer off the road, you endure a drop like that, you get to the bottom, car destroyed . . . you've got to be dead, right? You've GOT TO BE.

But I was alive.

When the police officers got there, they had a lot of questions.

"What happened? Did somebody run you off the road?"

"No sir."

"Did you lose control of the car?"

"No sir."

I answered honestly as I watched them load the wreckage of my car onto a tow truck. How did I feel at a moment like this? A little bit ashamed, honestly. All these people coming out here because of my stupid decision. I was also confused. I still couldn't get over WHY I WASN'T DEAD. It didn't make sense to me.

Next I had to contend with Eugene, who was so full of faith and always leading the most exemplary life. I hadn't really seen that example from a male before—at least not to that degree. He was stern with me. He said, "We've got to get you some help."

He meant SPIRITUAL help.

It would take a minute to feel the REDEMPTION, the knowledge that I was getting a second chance and there was really A WHOLE NEW LIFE ahead for me.

From practically that moment on, my life has never been the same. People talk about being saved. I was LITERALLY saved.

Moving Forward with Grace

After intending to commit suicide and getting a second chance, I've got a lesson for y'all.

Don't give up.

That's it—don't give up.

I was ready to quit. God had bigger plans for me. I don't know if that's everyone's outcome, but God ushered me down the side of that highway. Lo and behold, look what comes after that.

I've got a family of five kids, a new partner, new friends, a passion for coaching and helping young people, a whole new life I couldn't have even fathomed back then. There's so much life after what you think is your ending.

I put a period at the end of my sentence.

God erased that and replaced it with an exclamation point.

I know some of y'all can't sometimes see hope. You think it's over, but it's impossible to see your entire story. That's why you've GOT to keep going, no matter what. Because I'm telling you there's a whole other life out there, if you're open to it and choose that path.

I've told my team the story about the time I tried to take my life. They are usually pretty wide-eyed and silent as they're hearing those words. It's not a place I like to visit very often, but if it makes an impact on their lives, I'm happy to use it as a teaching tool.

Honestly, many of the things I did early in my life and career were teaching tools. I didn't wear a neck full of jewelry because I wanted to look like Mr. T, I wore it because I wanted to show my people back home in Fort Myers that you DIDN'T have to sell drugs to get to that level. Stay straight, work hard, and you can get things. I wanted to show that you didn't have to succumb to peer pressure.

I fell victim to different kinds of pressure. But when I got my second chance, I started asking myself different kinds of questions.

What am I?

Who am I?

I truly felt my kids were the only people who cared. Because I wasn't Prime to them. I was Daddy. That was my consistency in a life filled with inconsistencies.

My biggest challenge with accepting a life of faith was understanding the lies of all those people who pretended to be perfect. Look, all they had to do was tell me, "Hey, there's no such thing," and I would've been so advanced. I would have gained YEARS.

I guess that when it comes to the lies and inconsistencies, you've got to find that out for yourself. I finally learned the truth. God never called me to be PERFECT. He just called me to be PRESENT.

You know who finally told me the truth? It was Kirk Franklin, my guy, the rapper and songwriter, the man who gave me so much inspiration through his music, and whose music I was listening to that very night I tried to end it all. He befriended me and said, "Look man, I'm going to tell you this before we really kick it. I am NOT perfect. I'm not this. I'm not that. I'm just Kirk Franklin. God is still working on me. I've got a tremendous gift, but I am not perfect."

I just said, "Thank you, man," and I hugged him. We've been tight ever since.

I'm never perfect, but I'm always present.

It has been a process, and I don't want to say there was a turning point. But I had a remarkable, dramatic moment that clearly showed me my path.

Not long after I drove that car over the cliff, Eugene set me up with a guy he knew, Pastor David Forbes, and I opened up in a way I never had before. I asked Eugene what it meant to be a believer in Jesus, what it meant to be saved. Bishop T.D. Jakes, who had a huge ministry in Texas, began calling me. God sent all these people into my life.

I met up with Marc Logan, who was my teammate with the 49ers. He came to the ballpark in Cincinnati, then we went to IHOP and talked for hours. He asked me if I was saved. Eugene had been asking me the same thing. So, all of this was really weighing on my mind.

Why had Marc Logan come to Cincinnati and reached out to me? Why were all these people coming into my life and trying to help my situation? I realized this wasn't a coincidence.

When I went back to my hotel room, it was about four in the morning. What happened next was straight out of a movie. These awesome lights started flashing in my room and I was awakened.

I had been going through hell and felt like I was decaying. Now there were these bright lights in my room. It was like a 747 had landed beside my bed and there was this rush of wind, like a helicopter was landing.

I was in the presence of God. And I said, "God, I'm yours. I'm yours." I had never seen anything like that before—and I haven't since. I knew what it was. I fell to my knees. I was trembling all over. Then it got quiet and the lights disappeared.

I got up and opened the Bible. I randomly went right to Romans 10, verses 9 and 10.

If you confess with your mouth the Lord Jesus and believe in your heart that God has raised Him from the dead, you will be saved. For with the heart one believes unto righteousness, and with the mouth confession is made unto salvation.

I was destined to read those words. At that moment, I knew I had been saved.

The first person I called was Eugene. I told him what happened. I had a new beginning. Look, I realize everyone doesn't have a dramatic story like that. I guess for me, I needed something like that because drama had constantly been a part of my life. Truly, my life hasn't been the same since that moment. Don't get me wrong. I still have my trials and tribulations. It's not all perfect. But I know my direction. I know my destiny.

That's why I URGENTLY want you to know your direction and destiny. Because that's how you find your peace.

Stop Your Chase

It seems like all of us are chasing something.

Money? That's a BIG one, no doubt. How often do you dream about a larger salary, a promotion, hitting the lottery, being able to pay your bills, getting out of debt? Shoot, I once recorded a song called "It Must Be the Money," so cashing in was definitely once my version of God.

Fame? We all want adulation and praise. These days, we're after social media followers and viral videos. Some celebrities can't get enough of their television appearances and magazine articles. We all want to be loved and appreciated. It makes us feel so POWERFUL.

Sex? Professional athletes have UNBELIEVABLE access to women. There are temptations around every corner. We're all surrounded by what the Bible calls "sins of the flesh," and there's no doubt it's very challenging for young people. Marriages are threatened. Sex is constantly being confused with love.

There was a time when I thought money, fame, and sex were my life's biggest goals. But I learned the hard way, having endured years of pure EMPTINESS, that they were not. Now I know exactly what I'm chasing, but I'm not even sure if it's a "chase." It's more like a process, a way of living and being true to yourself.

Every day I want to find my peace.

That means LIVING my faith. That means APPRECIATING what I have. That means discovering JOY in my relationships and finding PURPOSE in my day-to-day routines.

If you maintain those qualities in your life, you have EVERY-THING.

My head coach at Florida State, Bobby Bowden, was a righteous man. He knew his priorities and he was consistently driven by his faith. But he was also a really competitive football coach. He got close to winning it all several times, only to be denied, over and over again. Many people wondered if he'd ever "win the big one."

After the 1993 season, when the Seminoles finally finished number one, Coach Bowden said the strangest thing happened. He compared it to climbing a mountain. When FSU was number one, Coach Bowden said he was happy to be at the pinnacle. After all those years, he reached the mountaintop. He looked around. And there was NOTHING there.

You visualize what it would be like to acquire the material possessions of your dreams. You wonder what it would feel like to reach the top of your profession. At that point, everything would be perfect . . . right? At least that's what we think.

Y'all ever have that feeling, and then find out it's not true?

You finally get that big raise, then you discover that more money can sometimes create more problems. You're promoted, but managing people turns out to be more of a headache than you ever imagined. You achieve everything you've ever dreamed about, but you just aren't happy. In fact, you're MISERABLE. It feels like your world is just swirling around and you have no control.

You need to find your peace. It might mean setting your priorities and sticking to them. It might mean simplifying your life. It might mean the understanding that your true joy is found in the process, not the achievement itself.

When my NFL career really got going, that was the time when I thought I had it all. I was moving through life at the speed of light. But really, I was just standing still. I saw so much emptiness. I actually saw rock bottom.

Rock bottom for me was having hundreds of suits in my closet but not relieving any of the pain. Rock bottom for me was having hundreds of pairs of shoes but I couldn't take a step in the right direction.

Rock bottom for me was having ten cars but not going anywhere. Rock bottom for me was having a fourteen-thousand-square-foot house but never feeling at home.

Rock bottom for me was lying between two and three women at a time but leaving unsatisfied. And lying right beside the person who said she loved me and her not even knowing I was in pain.

That was rock bottom to me.

What if you got more money than you can count, but chasing money is your god and your marriage is crumbling? What if you're a smooth-talking dude who's always working an angle, but your kids don't really know who you are because you're never home to guide them?

That is NOT winning.

You find your way up by pleasing God and helping other people. That's how you find your peace. I can promise you that if you're chasing material things, if you're chasing praise and adulation, you're going to reach a point where that no longer fulfills you or provides what you need. Finding your peace is the ANSWER.

Make Faith Your Foundation

When I was very young, I made some key decisions.

I stopped using profanity at nineteen. There was no purpose for it, so I stopped—cold turkey. You'll hear me say "darn" or "bull-junk," but that's as far as I take it. There's a lot of profanity that exists on the football field—and it ain't going away—but I made the decision to flush it.

As I've said many times before, I've never smoked, done drugs, or tasted alcohol in my entire life. My biological father did drugs and my stepfather drank. I knew those two forces all too well—and what they do to families, friends, and loved ones. I didn't want it and I didn't need it. People hear that and don't believe it, but it's TRUE. Just know that I was NOT under the influence of ANYTHING when I did all the stupid and idiotic things in my life. I was clean and sober when I made my mistakes. I surely don't need that stuff to give me some artificial feeling of happiness.

If you meet somebody who doesn't use profanity, doesn't smoke, and doesn't drink, what do you normally think? That has to be a Christian, right?

I wasn't always a person who claimed to know Jesus personally, but I knew where he was located and I didn't want to play with that. I was trying to get myself perfect, but all I was doing was delaying the process.

You see church folks and they have it all together, right? But it's never all together. If things were always perfect, would you really need Jesus? The Bible says there will always be tribulations and you should understand that. Realize that you were BUILT for these trials and you're NEVER going to be perfect, no matter how hard you try.

When you give yourself to the Lord, you find your peace. You don't care what people think of you. You're good. You live to please the Lord, not a man. Because a man (or woman) is NEVER going to be pleased. You can always come up short in their minds. So that should never be your mission or your journey.

If someone has a problem with you but God tells you, "Well done, my faithful servant," you should be good. You don't need anything more than that. You don't need hand claps from other people to feel better about yourself.

The world is filled with too many people-pleasers. We need more God-pleasers!

Following the Path

I'm at complete peace with the path I'm following in college football. I feel like the Lord is using me in different ways and the result is going to be something glorious.

Having that peace gets you to the next level of purpose with the Lord. You're better able to understand what He desires for you, whether that's unifying people or spreading His gospel.

Having that peace helps you to hear Him more clearly and it helps you to fully know the assignments He has for you.

Many people close to me never understood why I went to Jackson State. Or why I took the job at Colorado. I understood both perfectly. I'm building up to something bigger and earning a new assignment. I can be trusted at a major level and I'm making a different sort of impact. It was also God's plan. God called me collect and I accepted the charges.

Toward the end of my last season at Jackson State, I had contact with Colorado and some other schools. I hadn't gotten down the runway with a decision on what I was gonna do. I was having lunch with Andre Hart, my linebackers coach, and I heard a whisper.

Colorado.

Just a little whisper.

Colorado.

So, I called up Rick George, the Colorado athletic director. He took the call thinking it was going to be another round of me saying I'm not going to do it. But I just told him one thing.

I'm coming.

I told my coaches, "Look guys, this is what's going to happen. At the last minute, two other schools are going to come to us, and they will have outrageous financial numbers." And that's exactly what happened. Two schools came out of nowhere at the last minute and offered us a ton of money, significantly more. But I had already made up my mind with Colorado, and God had put me on the right path.

I think God wanted me on a whole different assignment, where I could bring notoriety and validation to a football program in a completely different way. He wanted me to unify people in a place with a Black school population of something like 3 percent. He wants me to change the game in a different way. It's not just about football, although WE ARE going to win. But this is not a simple-minded God. With the game He's playing, the scoreboard is much bigger than that.

Conversations with God

My conversations with God are not complicated.

For me, it's more like a personal relationship.

It's not memorizing a prayer or reciting lines. It's a CON-VERSATION, a heart-to-heart. With someone who I know will ALWAYS have my back.

Whatever I want to talk about, whatever I have on my plate, God already knows.

Even when I had my health issues at Jackson State, when I had all those surgeries and actually had to fight for my life, I never doubted for a second that God had my back. When you have trials in your life, you need to understand what's going on mentally, but completely trusting in God helps to expedite the process. At moments like that, you learn a lot about your faith. And hopefully, you'll see that your faith is where you think it should be.

If your life is threatened, always trust in God. Doubting Him should never be a moment in my mind. Bottom line: It's never just about you. It's about others learning from the lessons you articulate. I'm trying to articulate some lessons to you RIGHT NOW!

My understating and interpretation of faith isn't where God is dictating to us and telling us what to do. It's where we have a relationship with Him. And that's cool when you think about it. He's got my back. And He's got your back, too.

COACH PRIME'S TAKEAWAYS

1. **Everything starts with FAITH.** You can't be at your optimum without faith. For me, it's being a committed Christian and following God. Maybe you believe in a different higher power. But you need that faith-based guidance in your life.

2. **Faith has got to be a part of your DAILY life.** Y'all work out, right? You go to the gym or jump on your bike or lift some weights or run around the neighborhood or something like that? You do that to stay in shape. You've got to develop your faith muscles and keep them toned.

3. **Remember that faith isn't faith unless it's challenged—** and you still BELIEVE.

4. **When you have your faith in order, listen closely to find your peace.** Listen to your spirit. Is it whispering or yelling? If you don't truly feel at peace, you've got to identify what's wrong and be honest with yourself. If you're where you need to be, doing what you're supposed to do, your instincts will tell you the TRUTH.

5. **Always focus on the good side of things.** Being optimistic is going to be easier than staying negative. I tell people all the time to think about the best thing that can happen. Because if you keep pondering the worst thing, it WILL happen. Even when you're flat on your back— injured football players can relate to that very well— you've got to keep looking up.

How to Be Your OWN Coach

As the head coach at Colorado, I'm supposed to have all the answers, right? I make the calls, recruit the players, and decide who starts. And most of the time, that works just fine.

But there are days when I'm not sure about the answers. There are days when I need to reinforce my beliefs and charge my emotional batteries.

Before I can coach my players, I need to coach myself.

And you can do the same thing in your life.

When we began this book, I talked about being MORE than your coach. I would become your personal navigational system. We covered the twenty-one ways for you to win on and off the field, specific ways to ELEVATE your life so you can DOMINATE. I want you to keep using this book as your road map. Refer to it often. When you hit a bump in the road, these are the techniques to smooth things out.

How can you summon these concepts when you need them the most?

Here's a suggestion:

In my office at Colorado, I have a display of my favorite sayings and quotes, the words that can move me to action, the phrases that remind me what's really important. Why don't you do the same? Make some notes about the things you find motivating and relevant. Read them and reflect every day. When they become part of your consciousness, it won't be like learning a lesson. It will be your way of life.

I love my phrases.

Stay Right When the Crowd Goes Left.

Be unapologetically YOU. Don't feel compelled to do the expected if you have a better idea. Bring your unique side to the world.

Don't Allow My Confidence to Offend Your Insecurity.

Believe in yourself . . . always! If people have a problem with that, it's about them, not you.

A Play Don't Care Who Make It, So It Might As Well Be YOU!

If not you, then who? If not now, then when?

I Practiced Like I Played So When I Played It Was Like Practice.

Your success is based on what you do behind the scenes, when nobody is watching. Don't cheat the process.

My Calling Is Not Built on a Location, It's Built on a DESTINATION.

Keep the big picture in mind. Don't get hung up on a job title. Know your priorities and be true to them.

My Emotions Ain't Qualified to Make a Decision, but I AM.

Step back and think. You need a clear head and clear mind to make the big decisions.

The Man Never Tries to Be the Man Because That's WHO HE IS.

Don't brag about what you've got going on. Let others do the talking. Better yet, let your accomplishments tell the tale.

I Ain't Never Been One for Peer Pressure, but I Do Put PRESSURE on My Peers.

Follow your own path, but always stand for excellence.

I Don't Use Cologne Because Confidence Is My Natural Odor.

If you're prepared in the right way, you're gonna be ready for anything.

A Fan Only Blows When You're HOT.

Some days, you WON'T be on top of the world. Some days will be rough. Those are the days you need to endure, but don't stop working. Your day is coming.

A Cheetah Never Stretch Before He Go Get His Prey.

Don't hesitate. Be decisive. Don't get lost in a committee. You can dream, but eventually you've got to DO.

I LOVE the Life I LIVE . . . And I LIVE the Life I LOVE.

Do what you love. Find your calling. Discover your passion.

You Look Good, You Feel Good . . . You Feel Good, You Play Good . . . You Play Good, THEY PAY GOOD!

Dress for success. Prepare for success. When you do all the right things, the rewards are gonna follow.

I Was Called by God to Make a DIFFERENCE.

Don't settle for an average existence. Search for significance. Establish a legacy—and that could be as simple as making a difference in somebody else's life.

By my very nature, I have always been a controversial figure. That's OK. I enjoy that. But it has continued at Colorado, where we still have plenty of haters. I'll tell you this, though. We have a lot more believers than haters. We don't give the haters any kind of platform unless we're trying to make a point to the believers.

We don't acknowledge the hate. Because the love always outweighs the hate.

Always remember that, y'all. Sometimes you've got to live with the hate. But always remember to seek out the love.

You were never called to be average or typical. So let's get on with it. Every day find ways to ELEVATE your life. Pretty soon you're gonna DOMINATE. I believe in you. And I know you're gonna believe in yourself.

You got this!

ACKNOWLEDGMENTS

There are so many people that played a role in building this book that a list of all who should be acknowledged could go on for pages and pages.

I have wanted for many years to pull all these lessons together, but it was my longtime support team from SMAC Entertainment—Constance Schwartz-Morini, Jose Diaz, and Sam Morini—that really helped me take this from idea to reality. They worked with the great team at Simon & Schuster's 13A and Gallery Books imprints, led by Charles Suitt and Jen Bergstrom, with editing by Pamela Cannon, publicity by Lauren Carr, and marketing by Bianca Ducasse. Together they built the framework for the project and helped see it through to its excellent publication. A key to building this book was choosing writer Don Yaeger, who spent hours interviewing me and building those conversations into the framework.

None of these life lesson stories would be possible without my family. Connie Knight, my mama, has always been my rock, and my sister, Tracie, knows me better than anyone. Raising my kids—Deiondra, Deion Jr., Shilo, Shedeur, and Shelomi—has been my greatest joy.

All my kids have a special place in my heart, and they all serve a crucial role in this JOURNEY, but I would specifically like to call out my oldest son, Bucky, for the many hours of amazing content on his YouTube channel, Well Off Media. He has led the charge running my social media and has changed the landscape of sports and social media. Giving access to both Bucky and the Coach

Prime documentary team (that few ever get in a Big-Time athletic program) has allowed the world to see what we set out to build, both at Jackson State and at Colorado. This is much more than just football, this is LIFE!

When I think about becoming a coach, I have to credit the leaders who helped shape me: Dave Capel, Ron Hoover, and Bobby Bowden, along with the men who have worked alongside me since the beginning, Reginald Calhoun, Ray Forsett, Andre Hart, and Kevin Mathis.

My spiritual advisors, Bishop Omar Jahwar and Pastor E. Dewey Smith, gave me inspiration. I owe the world to my longtime agent, Eugene Parker, God rest his soul.

And lastly, to my athletic directors—Ashley Robinson and Rick George—thank you for BELIEVING in the vision and allowing me the opportunity to carry out my mission.

I say often that many of the greatest things accomplished happened because a team came together. This book is proof of that.